P9-DVV-625

Polly Prindle's Book of American Patchwork Quilts

Polly Prindle's Book of American Patchwork Quilts

BY ALICE I. GAMMELL
Revisions by Patricia Newkirk

GROSSET & DUNLAP
A FILMWAYS COMPANY
Publishers • New York

Text © 1973, 1976 by Alice I. Gammell
Black and white photographs © 1973 by Alice I. Gammell
Line drawings and color photographs © 1973 by Grosset & Dunlap, Inc.

Cover © 1976 by Grosset & Dunlap, Inc.

All rights reserved
Published simultaneously in Canada
Library of Congress Catalog Card Number: 72-92371
ISBN: 0448-01332-0

Printed in the United States of America

Foreword

At the age of eight I finished my first quilt, a bright red and white combination of squares and triangles. I then made the one quilt that would become a keepsake to me. This quilt was proof of my eagerness to work with prints in making interesting designs, especially those demanding odd scrap pieces, which held the most fascination for me. The swatches left from mother's aprons or brother's blouses held pleasant memories while fulfilling the desire to create designs calling for various colors. Today the urge for color in materials propels me to the yard goods counters on every shopping trip. The rows of gay prints on display always afford much interest for me.

Miss Polly of the title is my memory picture of a tiny girl painstakingly learning the elements of good seaming. These early achievements were due to the careful guidance of my mother, to whom I wish to dedicate this book.

I wish to acknowledge my indebtedness to Violet George, who so ably assisted me with the drawings, and to my daughter, who unselfishly gave of her time and effort in helping me with this work.

It is my hope that this book will be an incentive to others to become interested in quilts and quiltmaking. They too may learn that quilts are fun to make, lovely to look at and a pleasure to own.

Contents

MAKING A QUILT

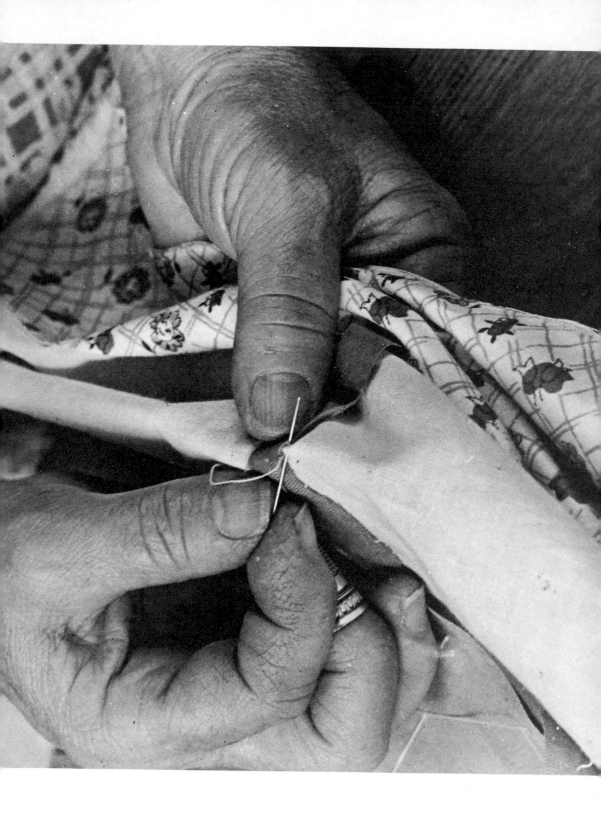

Patchwork's Past

Quiltmaking, both appliqué and pieced or patchwork, originated from the necessity for warm coverings. The original purpose remains valid but from time to time other ideas have been added, such as beauty of design, color effects, quilting and many others. These things have made the quilt world what it is today.

Not only does appliqué or patchwork provide a pleasing pastime, it also adds beauty, comfort and decoration in the form of hangings, cushions and clothing as well as quilts. It possesses charm in all its forms for every room in the house.

Quiltmaking has never lost its interest and fascination. It has always been held in high esteem, and is today being revived with more zest than at any time in its history. Many books and articles have been written on this most interesting subject, and as we read we marvel at the progress quiltmaking has made during its reign. Quiltmaking is believed to have originated in the Far East in the eleventh century. It was brought west by the returning Crusaders and gradually gained favor through Europe. Appliqué work appeared nearly everywhere and was designed in hundreds of different ways, being used in all forms and manners. Banners carried in battle displayed large bold emblems and patriotic symbols. Wall hangings were asplendor with vivid, intricate handworked designs. Bed drapes were also elaborate with handwork. The craft kept growing and soon coverlets were adorned and displayed with marvelous examples.

During the reign of Queen Elizabeth of England the ladies of the court did a great deal of this fine handwork as a pastime. It is also recorded that Queen Elizabeth's own wardrobe was elaborately decorated with handwork, a great deal of which she did herself. During Napoleon's reign appliqué was very much in vogue in France and pieced work was also

1

popular. Bold, daring designs were the most extensively used at that time, bespeaking the atmosphere of Do and Dare. A great deal of the old-time handwork has been preserved, and many of our art museums display this work of the past.

Some appliqué and patchwork took years to accomplish; as new designs made their appearance the plainer, simpler designs were replaced with ones that were more complex.

We as American women can feel that our grandmothers contributed greatly to the growth of quiltmaking. They were a thrifty generation of housewives and had more than a small share in creating the quilt patterns we have today. The original idea may have come to them from the Far East, but it was they who designed and introduced so many of the lovely patterns we know. Our grandmothers would create new designs by rearranging the pattern pieces and adding another simply shaped unit. There was a high degree of satisfaction in knowing that a new pattern had been created and they could be justly proud of their achievement.

Our ancestors valued their quilts not only for their beauty and comfort but because they were a source of self-expression that would live on and on, to be handed down from mother to daughter. These quilts were studies in thrift, economy and skill. The patterns exemplified wise planning and effective color arrangement and were the center of picturesque industry in this field. Every woman who made or designed her first quilt had the satisfaction of knowing she had created an article of lasting interest. It was so in accord with its surroundings that it was bound to be treasured for all time.

We owe our grandmothers more than a passing thought in this matter of quiltmaking. They could not send, phone or go to a department store and obtain just the shade they required. They had more to do; they spun the yarns at home, wove and dyed the materials. This in itself was an art, for the right shades were not easy to obtain. Dull browns, grays and similar colors were about the only available hues. Time, patience and perseverance were the only answers to their problems, yet they enjoyed finding creative solutions. Those women of yesterday created things of lasting beauty under the most trying conditions.

Thus we owe a great deal to the spinning wheel that was so deftly managed by our thrifty grandmothers. Those first quilts were made of heavier materials than we use today, yet the work was marvelously done. Although warmth was the main factor, beauty was also stressed, and many a housewife would beam with joy as she displayed a beautiful coverlet that she herself had designed and made.

Nearly all of these earlier quilts were marvelous examples of creative craftsmanship. Accuracy was of supreme importance. Their construction was correct in detail and fine workmanship, but their artistic beauty was also a thing to admire.

In the old days no hurried cutting or sewing was done. This part was considered to be of extreme importance, and young girls were taught the most exacting methods. Thus no materials were wasted from incorrect work. All women found time to do a certain amount of this work, most of them because they found it pleasurable — and all families needed what the housewife could manage to make. The art was so popular that groups of women met at designated places at stated times, each and every one doing her work or helping some friend complete her coverlet.

Perhaps a bride-to-be would be favored with a finished quilt, each block being done by women who really knew how. In those early days, dances, movies and other diversions did not exist to fill a young lady's life. After she was a grown woman and whispers linked her name with a certain gentleman, she busied herself with things for her future home. A bride's chest was a must and was supposed to contain a baker's dozen of quilts: twelve were for ordinary use and the thirteenth would be very elaborate. At quilting bees for brides the guests pieced a "Bride's Quilt" top, ending the festive day with an evening of dancing. The bride-to-be was presented with the quilt and was much envied by her friends.

These quilting bees of the earlier days were events that were looked forward to with much anticipation and enthusiasm. They were all-day events with each woman bringing along some dish of food to spell off the entertaining housewife: some would bring homemade butter, others would bake bread or rolls to be enjoyed by all. The day sped by all too quickly with much knowledge exchanged and perhaps a bit of gossip as nimble fingers accomplished a goodly amount of work.

Quilting bees were not the only form of gathering related to making quilts; cutting bees were also special events. The women of the neighborhood would meet just as they did for quilting, but in the cutting bees each one brought along her pattern and pieces. There was an exchange of pieces in cases where a woman had more light than dark and wished for a wider range of colors. The day was thus made more interesting and the quilts in question more colorful. At the cutting bees many new designs were created. A new design was the most exciting discovery imaginable, and a completed quilt the vital concern of all present.

It took no lavish spending to supply color and charm. A few odd bits of gay calico would supply all the bright features needed to set off the dull grays, browns or black prints used so extensively in the designs created by our pioneer grandmothers. They often led harsh lives and were faced with problems that demanded real thinking. Quilting and cutting bees were pleasant diversions that combined useful work with friendly chatter.

A list of quilt names arouses interest and creates a spirit of imagination that links the past to the present and rekindles all the thrills that

3

brightened the days of our ancestors. From the start quilt names were given to every design. During Napoleon's reign the "Star of France" made its appearance, and the "King's Crown" as well as the "Queen's Crown" were created. Many of the old much-used and beloved patterns were named for some special occasion. A spectacular event would inspire a new design with a brand-new name; thus we have "Pleasant Paths," "Ships at Sea," "Sugar Bowl" and many others. Political events ranged high in inspiring new names, "Road of the White House," "Georgetown Circle" and "Lincoln's Platform" being only a few. Flowers were an inspiring element, with "Rose of Sharon," "Democrat Rose," "Dutch Rose," "Tulip," "Rose Wreath," "Jonquil," "Pansy" and many more in this category. The old-time dances were also the source of many names, such as "Virginia Reel" and "Grand Right and Left." "Floral Bouquet" was designed and named by a young lady who had made a dress for a special dance. At this dance she met her future husband. She immediately set about making a coverlet using the scrap pieces from this dress as the main color in her quilt.

A number of the interesting designs that hold one's attention are designed from and named after stars, perhaps because of the mystery that accompanies the star. We have the "Blazing Star," "Star of Texas," "Eight-Pointed Star," "Orphan Star" and "Rolling Star," to cite only a few of the hundreds of star designs. Other names held in high favor are "Harvest Moon," "Rising Sun," "Tea Leaf," "House that Jack Built," "Mary's Fan," "Goose Tracks" and "Horn of Plenty." Thus it is apparent that countless things, both animal and mineral, have supplied names for many of our most interesting patterns. The names of many designs have changed as time has passed. Perhaps a slight change in color arrangement brought out a different look in the design and immediately a new name was invented.

Today the keen interest being shown in this art proves that Americans have always followed in the footsteps of their ancestors. We can be justifiably proud of the part our grandmothers had in creating the lovely designs we so much admire today. We can also be proud of our modern versions, with the augmented colorings used in our newer patterns. We know the coverlets we have made, and plan to make, will go down in history as keepsakes made and loved by true American women.

Eight Steps for Making a Quilt

1. Choose your pattern and materials.
2. Make the pattern and cut out the pattern units. If the pattern given shows a fold, make the pattern full size rather than cut the fabric on the fold. This makes pieces more accurate. If directions call for cutting half the pieces "facing left" and half "facing right," do so by turning the pattern wrong side up for half of them. This is a must if your fabric has a right and a wrong side.
3. Sew the quilt blocks.
4. Join the blocks together, with or without sashing. Sashing is also known as *lattice*.
5. Attach a border.
6. Arrange the quilt top, filler and backing in place on the quilt frame.
7. Quilt or tie your coverlet.
8. Attach an edging or binding.

Parts of a Quilt

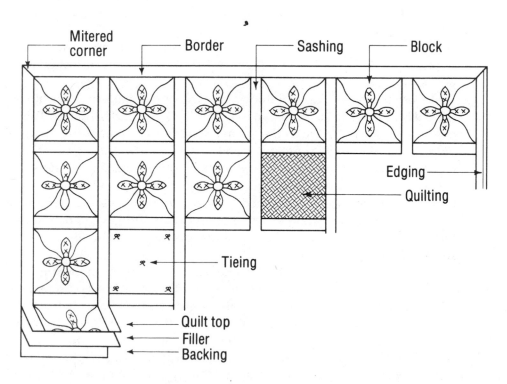

5

1. Choose Your Pattern and Materials

Your Pattern

There are many things to take into consideration when you plan to make a quilt. Are you to use scrap pieces that have accumulated in your piece bag? Does the room where the quilt is to be used need color and beauty? Are you capable of making an intricate design or must it be a beginner's pattern? Is your time limited? All these and many more things must be thought out and your quilt planned accordingly.

If your room is furnished in antiques, consider one of the old-type patterns that our grandmothers made. "Job's Tears" is not difficult and was a design much used in the old days. The "Log Cabin" with its many different versions is another of the old easy-to-make designs. The "Six-Pointed Star" is a lovely thing to own. These and many more of the old-type designs would make beautiful additions to rooms furnished with period furniture.

Modern rooms call for an entirely different kind of pattern. Many times the only color in such a room is in the coverlets, rugs and hangings. These must add beauty and life to the room. Here you should choose a large, bold, bright design with plenty of color. A pattern with colors that add charm and warmth will repay its owner manyfold in satisfaction and joy.

A large, bold pattern may run riot in a room with plain walls, but flowered, conspicuous walls need a more subdued design. Perhaps a simple appliquéd design on a neutral-color background would be just the thing. All these aspects add up to a coverlet well in keeping with its surroundings.

Do you wish to make a quilt for some particular person? In the present-day quilt world you can find patterns to suit all individuals. Ships and airplanes for the young men, sunbonnet girls and animals for the little tots, fish designs for the man of the house, flowers and ever so many more things for you, both to admire and to display to your friends.

Limited time may demand that you choose a simple, straight-line pattern. This may be made by machine, thus saving time; with care the

Opposite: The Red Schoolhouse

6

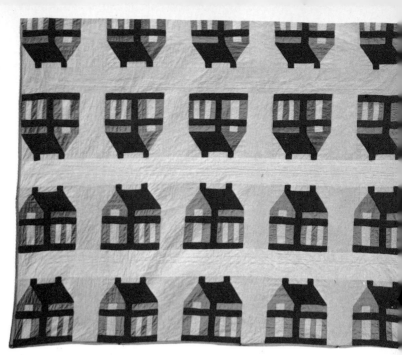

The Red Schoolhouse
(Pattern on page 148)

Job's Tears
(Pattern on page 210)

Opposite:
Patchwork Flower

Detail of Patchwork Flower,
showing use of sashing
fabric for backing

Patchwork Flower
(Pattern on page 194)

corners will "miter" as well as if made by hand. However more time must be given to the joining if the quilt is made by machine. If the work is done by hand the seams may be adjusted as the sewing progresses. When done by machine the edges may stretch, and this may pass unnoticed until the seams are completed. This will result in a poorly made block, and the seams must be ripped out, the units pressed and the block remade.

There is far too much thought, work and anticipation involved to run the risk of an unsatisfactory product, so why not plan ahead and from the very start decide to go slowly. You will have a finished article that will be a joy forever.

Hundreds of quilt patterns as well as quilting patterns are available to quilt lovers. These designs are the product of extensive study by quilt lovers from all parts of the world. From the time the first quilt was made to today, with a few touches of individual tastes, new aspects to already interesting patterns have been created. We have unlimited ideas to work with in this field.

In this book are fifty well-known patterns for quilt blocks and a handful of patterns for borders. With thought and imagination you can easily devise your own variations once you have learned some basics.

Color Arrangement

Before you venture very far into quiltmaking you must map out a color scheme that will fit the materials to be used. To some the arrangement of color might seem like a minor detail, but whether you are to use odd scraps or new goods bought specially for your quilt, a planned arrangement will prove to be the most satisfactory.

What will be accomplished if you do not adhere to the rules? An article with a poor color balance will never be a comfort because it never can be good looking. A haphazardly designed quilt will probably be tucked away in a place of seclusion and classed as an expensive failure, not only from the actual cost of materials, but from the viewpoint of labor and disappointment. On the other hand, picture the joy and pride you will have in displaying to your friends an article that is well planned and well made.

For a well-balanced quilt there must be a set idea carried out throughout the entire quilt top. On flowered quilts, for example, stems should be all one shape and color, while flower petals may be different colors providing all the centers are of one color. Leaves may be of a different shade from the stems but should be the same as each other.

It is true that every individual has her own ideas on the setting together of colors. A quilt that would appear a gorgeous affair to one may be

An effective design is created by dark ships on a light background.

considered poor by another. Each one therefore must make an arrangement to suit her own fancy.

Here you can find a link to the past if you consider the colorings that our grandmothers used. If you are planning an old-time design you naturally want the effect to be as near the original colorings as possible. Present-day stores carry a line of materials that resemble the older type of goods, so your selection is not difficult.

It must be remembered that in all designs the darker colors will stand out against the lighter shades, so if a definite element is to be stressed that particular part of the design or block should be made of the darker fabric. For example, in the "Necktie" design, you naturally want the "tie" to be the important element. Therefore you should use the dark for the "tie" and the lighter goods for the remainder of each block. To use the example of the "Ship" design, the dark ships skimming along in a background of light blue will bring out every block to a marked degree, but if those same ships were of a light shade they would not be half as noticeable.

If you want the background to match some particular color arrangement, make it of a dark color. You'll notice that when such a quilt is displayed the shade or color of the background will be commented on prior to any mention of the design, which again shows that the darker color makes the first impression.

Many who are in doubt about which colors are most suitable to a design prefer to cut and make a block of some material of no special consequence before actually cutting the material they are to use in their quilt. This has proven to be a very good plan, as then there is no doubt as to just what the color effect will be.

Fabric

Whether you use scrap pieces or purchase new materials, the rule of only soft-textured, wash-fast materials must be followed. Inferior goods lead only to disappointment. Harsh materials are difficult to quilt; loosely woven goods have a tendency to stretch and no amount of care will remedy this factor. The disappointment one may experience if inferior goods are used can be measured only in wasted time. Many times such quilts are never fully completed. So give your materials plenty of thought and choose only soft, closely woven goods for best results. Percale is the material most commonly used. Good-quality ginghams, sateen, calico, broadcloth or chintz are other worthwhile fabrics.

Scrap materials can be made into as beautiful a quilt as though all new materials had been purchased. With careful planning one can derive great charm from the accumulation of odd pieces that are found in nearly every home. Of course the pattern must suit the purpose, but with so many odd-scrap designs available it is not difficult to make a good selection. No piece of material, no matter how small, need be wasted as there is a design for every need. There is no exception. All material that is fast to washing can be used and made into a quilt of beauty and distinction.

One of the designs created especially for using odd scraps is the "Crazywork." Cutting is needed only to trim off irregular edges. The pieces, regardless of shape, are used "as is" and are hemstitched to a background square of any desired size. The pieces should overlap at the edges just enough to prevent the seams from fraying out. Pieces are fitted in at any angle as long as the background is entirely covered. This kind of odd-scrap work has many advantages that no other design can boast of. It may be sashed or not. A border may or may not be used. Background patches may be cut all one size, or they may be of different sizes. At the time of finishing they may be sewn in strip fashion and joined with or without a plain strip between each pieced portion. A new version has alternating blocks of plain material between crazywork blocks.

Another good feature is that the background may serve as the back. If extra weight is desired, however, a filler may be used. In either case the quilt will look equally well whether it is tied or quilted. Thus we have one of the most liberated designs imaginable. Not many designs can boast of so much interest and so many good qualities.

2. Make the Patterns and Cut Out the Pattern Units

What to use as a pattern for the pieces of each square has been a source of worry to most quiltmakers. If you use paper patterns, the edge is gradually cut away as the pattern is used over and over. If paper is to be used, several patterns should be cut at the same time. As the cutting progresses, the used patterns can be discarded and replaced by the ones held in reserve.

Sandpaper has proved to be a much better material to use. Because of its thickness it will not get cut down in size as you use it. If laid face down against the material it will hold fast to its position, thus eliminating pinning the pattern to the goods. Blotting paper has also been used extensively as a cutting guide, as it also adheres to the material, making cutting time easier and faster. You can also use plastic with double-stick tape.

Be exact in cutting, and do not waste materials. Put your patterns on the material as close together as possible, making sure to place the pattern units on the straight grain of your fabric. If you are not confident of your ability to estimate the ¼-inch seam allowance when stitching the pattern units together, mark the sewing line on the units as you cut them out. Then clip or string all the identical pieces together so you will not lose them.

3. Sew the Quilt Blocks

Patchwork

Patchwork, or pieced work, is the art of joining pieces of material together to form a design. A straight running stitch is used to join the pattern pieces into a block, and then the blocks are sewn together to form the entire quilt top.

In the early days of quiltmaking, many quilts were made of patchwork squares. Various scraps of colored and patterned materials were cut into small squares and joined together, eighteen squares making one block. The size of the squares would determine the size of the blocks and thus the number of blocks needed and the size of the finished quilt top.

Today we have hundreds of beautiful patterns that combine squares, triangles and many other shapes into pieced blocks. These designs can be easy to make, with straight seams and few units, such as "The Spool" and "The Ship Quilt," or as complicated as the rare and beautiful "Baby Bunting" or the lively "Red Schoolhouse."

Appliqué

Appliqué work in quiltmaking is done by placing a chosen motif or arranging several motifs on an oblong or square piece of plain cloth. After

arranging this motif you baste it into place. The next step is to take your sewing needle and turn in all raw edges on your motif by using a fine hemming stitch. After you have completed this hemming work you will have one finished block.

Appliqué allows us to make many delicate designs, including "Sunbonnet Sue," "Rose of Sharon" and "Blossoms and Berries," as well as all-over patterns such as "Job's Tears." Designs such as "Grecian Star" and "Dresden Plate" combine both pieced work and appliqué to further enrich the quiltmaker's art.

4. Join the Blocks Together, With or Without Sashing

Many means are used to connect the blocks. Sashing is the one most extensively used (see below). Another method of arranging blocks is to alternate the patterned blocks with blocks of plain material the same size as the patterned block.

If you are using a fairly simple pattern, you can alternate pattern blocks with blocks made of a print that appears in the pattern. The drawing of a completed "Sunbonnet Sue" quilt top illustrates one possible arrangement. When plain blocks are alternated with patterned blocks they may be placed in many different positions, giving the quilt an entirely new aspect. Diagonal placement of the patterned blocks makes a pleasing appearance. If only a few patterned blocks are wanted, a larger amount of plain material may be used, spacing the blocks throughout the quilt top. The different aspects of block arrangement can be mastered with a bit of study and forethought.

Sashing

Sashing, although not necessary, adds distinction and prestige to a quilt and should be given much consideration. It is especially appropriate with the new appliquéd designs that have found their way into the quilt world in recent years. Most — in fact nearly all — of these new creations look best with varied and colorful sashings and borders. Many of them owe their popularity to the thought given to the arrangement of color and design in these final touches.

Sashing should be used to separate individual blocks that stand out by themselves. It is not used with all-over designs. Many pieced patterns form a sashing as each block is made, so extra sashing is not needed.

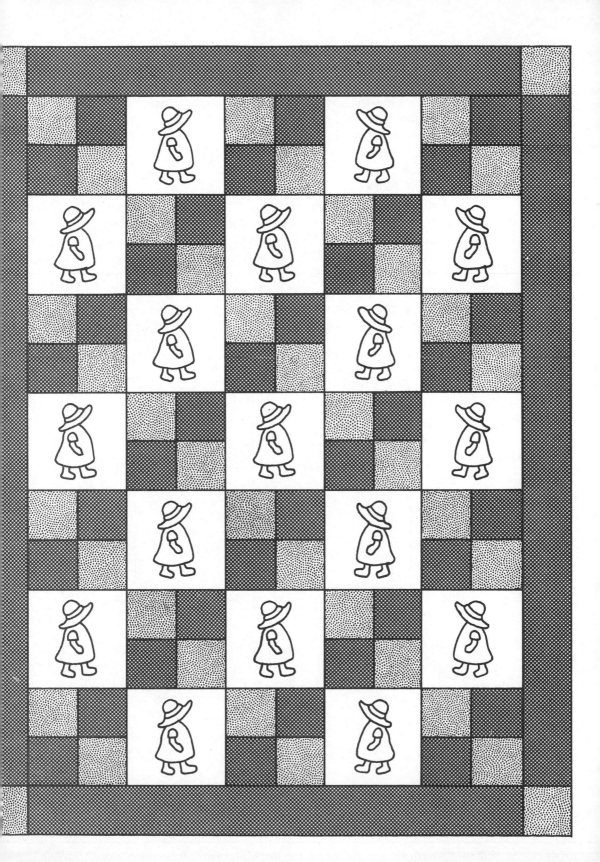

Sashing is usually 2½ inches wide, although some designs may look equally well with a 2-inch or even a 3-inch sashing. Some of the patterns in this book allow for sashing, but many do not. If you plan to add sashing to a quilt that does not specify sashing in the instructions remember to adjust the number of blocks so your quilt will be the right size. To make the sashing, cut strips of material the width you desire, remembering to allow ¼ inch on each side for the seam allowance. Strips are first cut the width of the blocks and are sewn to the top and bottom of each block with a running stitch, making strips of blocks the desired width of the quilt top. Next you must cut or piece together strips the length of the quilt; these are then sewn to the rows of blocks. In this way you will connect your blocks on the width and length into one quilt top.

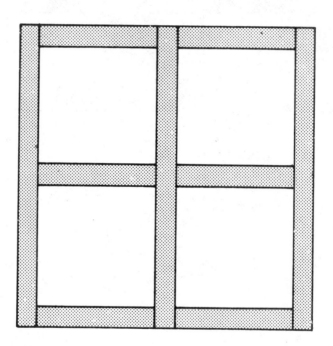

Two colors are often used in a sashing, especially in the newer designs. One attractive method of combining two colors is to place a square of the second color at each corner of the blocks.

If the blocks have large areas of a plain background color, the sashing may be made of squares of all different figured and plain materials. This is an ideal way to use the odd scraps left from cutting the block pattern units.

Take care to choose sashing materials that harmonize with and complement your blocks. You will often find that repeating colors from the pattern blocks will work best. Be sure never to use a figured sashing when blocks are of figured materials, as you do not want your sashing to detract from or compete with the pattern blocks.

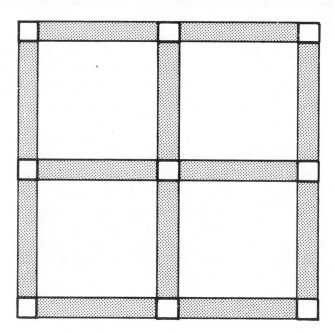

5. Attach a Border

After joining the blocks you are ready to attach a border. Your border may be as plain or as elaborate as you desire. Take into account your ability and the time available before you venture into this phase of finishing your quilt.

The border should be in keeping with the overall design of your quilt. A quilt with sashing will usually look best with a border of the same material and width used for the sashing. Just cut four strips of fabric equal to the length and width of your finished quilt top, miter the corners and sew the border to the quilt top.

Attractive borders can also be made by using plain strips of the same material used in the pattern blocks. You can combine two colors, one of which may be the color used for the background or for alternating plain squares.

In some cases when quilts are finished with a border but found to be a little small for the individual requirements, a plain outside border is added. This is also very effective with quilts that have scalloped edges.

Borders can also repeat pattern motifs such as triangles or diamonds that appear in the quilt top. More elaborate designed borders can also be made from the patterns given in this book.

The border is as important as the quilt top itself. You should give much thought and consideration as to the proper design to use, the correct width for balance, and the right colors to harmonize with the surroundings.

Five Steps to Miter a Corner

1. Lay material to be mitered on cutting table with right side of material up.

2. Measure length of material needed. Allow ½ inch extra material to give ¼-inch hem on each end.

3. Cut each end of material at a 45-degree angle.

4. Fold ¼-inch hemming material under and press with iron.

5. Repeat for second piece of material and sew together to form a 90-degree angle.

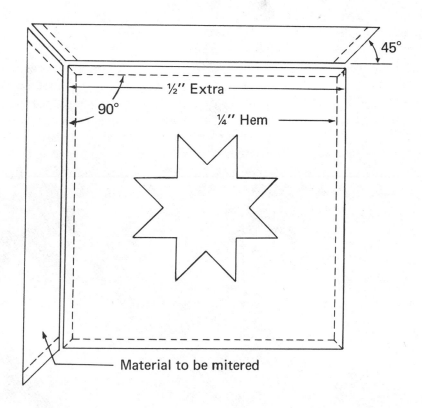

45°

½" Extra

90°

¼" Hem

Material to be mitered

6. Arrange the Quilt Top, Filler and Backing in Place on the Quilt Frame

After the quilt top is completed, it is attached to the filler and quilt back by means of quilting or tieing. Usually when a cotton batting or filler is used, close quilting is done, with the rows of stitches not more than one inch apart. This allows frequent washings with no danger of separation of the fibers of the batting.

Polyester or dacron fillers are the best to use, even though the cost is a little higher than cotton batting. The polyester filler tends to withstand laundering much better than the cotton batting. Some quilters do prefer cotton batting, however, as they feel a polyester filler makes quilting more difficult. Cotton blankets may also be used for the filler, especially with tied quilts.

The quilt back should be made of material that will harmonize with the top; most quilters repeat either the main background color or sashing material for the back. It is best to have the backing a trifle larger than the quilt top, because when the top and back are pulled taut, the seaming of the top will allow for a bit more stretching than can be obtained from the plain material used for the back.

Most quilters use a frame to hold the quilt while the quilting is being done. There are folding frames on the market today that may be purchased at most needlecraft supply stores. These vary in size and quality, and a homemade device may serve equally well. To make a frame, first obtain four boards with planed and straight edges. These should be ⅝ inch thick and 2½ inches wide. Two of the boards should be 84 inches long and the other two 110 inches long. Boards of this length will accommodate nearly

A finished quilt top is pinned to a quilting frame.

all lengths of quilts. Holes should be bored starting 3 inches from each end of the four boards and continuing to a length of about 18 inches; these holes allow you to adjust the frame for different-sized quilts. Four bolts with wing nuts are needed to hold the frame intact. A strip of strong cloth is tacked to the inside edge of each board for sewing or pinning the material to the frame. The tacks should be placed rather close together so the quilt will not sag after it is on the frame. The boards are placed on chair backs or similar objects, one at each corner, at the height desired for comfort while quilting. The next step is to square one corner of the frame and bolt it firmly. The back of the quilt is pinned or sewn completely to the end board with the wrong side of the material facing up. The opposite side is then pinned in place, the material pulled tightly and the remaining three corners of the frame squared and bolted. The two sides are then pinned, and the back is now ready for the filler. This is laid on the quilt back and smoothed out so no thick places are to be found. Any thick spots will make quilting difficult and stitches uneven. After the filler is firmly in place the quilt top can be pinned. This is done in the same way as the quilt back, pinned to each end and then the sides. Long basting stitches will help to hold the top in place (see below).

Quilt top, filler and back are basted together.

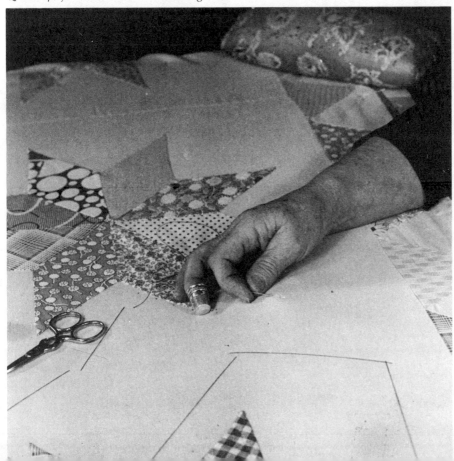

You are now ready to proceed with the quilting. Two small clamps will come in handy to replace the two corner bolts at the end where the quilting is being done. As the work progresses the sides are unpinned and the part of the quilt that has been quilted is rolled around the end pole. If you cannot purchase the small clamps, holes may be bored the full length of the boards and the bolts used for the entire process.

Should you wish to use a quilting hoop, you may first assemble the quilt on the frame. Then baste it in a haphazard fashion over the entire surface and remove it from the frame.

Hoops are very simple to use and convenient when room space is limited. These hoops are like large embroidery hoops and are used extensively, as they require only a small space the size of a sewing table and

Quilting by using a quilting hoop.

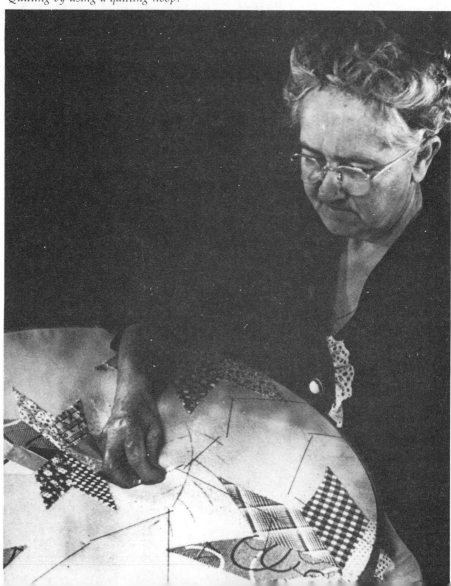

can be taken from one room to another. Twenty-two inches in diameter is the usual size to use. To use the hoop the quilt is laid on a table, after being removed from the large frame, and the hoop is placed on the upper left-hand corner of the quilt just as one would use an embroidery hoop. A screw on the hoop will adjust it for different weights in materials. Tighten the hoop to the thickness of your quilt and you are now ready to start the quilting. These hoops, like the frames, may be purchased at most needlecraft supply stores.

Adjusting the quilting hoop.

7. Quilt or Tie Your Coverlet

Quilting

Quilting designs can be worked out with little difficulty even by the inexperienced. The main reason for quilting is to hold the top, filler and the back intact through repeated washings. A second reason is for the decorative qualities. Many quiltmakers prefer a plain material for the top and back without any appliqué or pieced work in order to have fancy quilting displayed to its fullest.

The quilting will require some planning, time and effort. Straight quilting is nothing more than a running stitch like plain sewing, with the stitches as short as possible. The amount of quilting to be done will depend on the ability of the quilter, the design and the kind of filler that is used. Quilting, like the quilt top, may be very simple or as elaborate as the individual desires. For those unfamiliar with this work a simple design will be the best, especially for a first attempt. It must be remembered that the most simple design can be decorative, yet not too difficult for the beginner.

Straight quilting is nothing more than a running stitch.

To quilt your coverlet you should use quilting thread, any color, or size forty or fifty waxed thread with a short, sharp needle (a quilting needle is usually a "betweens" size 7, 8 or 9) that permits you to make very short stitches. For an attractive, simple finish you can quilt the entire surface of your quilt top with short running stitches about one inch apart on both the length and width. This style of quilting is often used on patchwork quilts.

Your quilting pattern should be in keeping with your design. Quilting around particular design elements will give them a raised effect. If you have appliquéd your quilt top, for example, you can follow the appliquéd design of each block with short running stitches and then finish the background with close quilting. This can be done in straight quilting, crosses or in a square effect as you wish. The quilting patterns shown on the following page can be used for many different kinds of quilt tops. Any kind of quilting will add to the beauty and charm of your coverlet, and the close quilting will eliminate any future washing troubles.

When quilting in this fashion you sew down through the quilt top, filler and backing so the stitching shows on both the top and back of the finished quilt. Don't leave knots on the surface because they are unsightly. Make small knots and pull them through the top thickness to the

While right hand moves needle above the quilt, left hand guides needle below quilt.

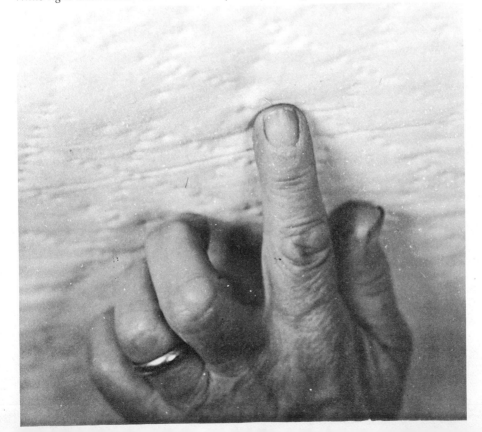

filler. A medium-length thread is best — a longer thread will twist and knot, demanding extra time and causing annoyance. The end of each needleful should be finished with several back stitches to hold the end firmly. These will not show and will add to the life of your quilt.

Quilting Patterns

Methods of Transferring Quilting Designs

If the quilting design is simple, cardboard patterns can be used very successfully. Cut the pattern in the desired shape and then trace around it with a lead pencil. After the quilting is done pencil marks may be removed from quilts by gently rubbing over the marks with stale breadcrumbs. Many department stores or art supply stores sell art gum erasers that may be used to remove quilting lines.

A compass or ruler can also be used to draw the design on the quilt top with a pencil. Many simple designs can be traced or drawn successfully by this method.

Pierced patterns have been used in many cases, and with care these can be made very satisfactorily by the inexperienced. The pattern is first traced on a piece of plain white paper, then pierced with a needle. The pattern is then placed on the material to be quilted and stamped with stamping paste or powder, which is sold at most department stores. Directions for using the stamping material come with the paste or powder.

Transferring a design using dressmaker's carbon paper.

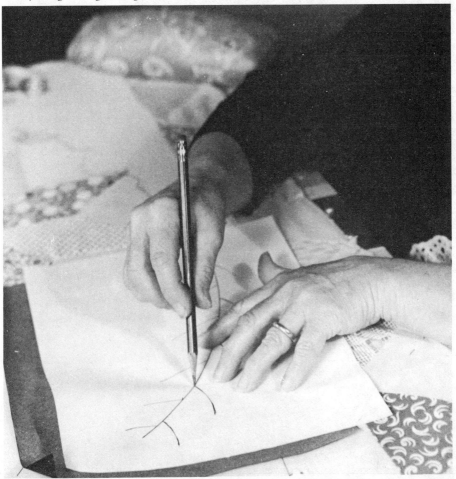

The quilting pattern can also be drawn or traced on thin paper, basted to the place to be quilted and the quilting done right through the paper. The paper is then torn away as the work progresses. This method is not used as extensively as others but is well worth trying.

Another way to transfer quilting designs is by first tracing or drawing the design on plain white paper. The design can be carefully followed by using an unthreaded sewing machine with a medium stitch. The pattern is then placed on the place to be quilted and lightly dusted with ground cinnamon. The cinnamon will adhere to the material sufficiently for the quilting and can then be brushed off. This method may be used repeatedly.

Quilting designs may also be transferred to the quilt top by using dressmaker's carbon for tracing. Should you choose this method, check

Pierced pattern is dusted with ground cinnamon.

to be sure that the carbon marks will wash out by first tracing on scraps of the same material you used to make the top. Then, trace your design *lightly*.

Cinnamon is rubbed over the pattern.

The pattern, now transferred to the quilt top, is quilted.

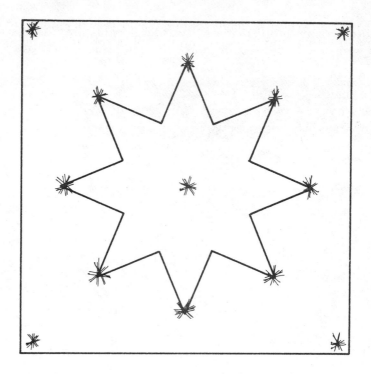

Tieing

A tied quilt demands less time than a quilted one and also has its good points.

The first step is to take your sewing needle with size fifty thread and make one stitch down through your quilt top, filler and backing and then back up, leaving about two inches of thread on the surface of your quilt. Make two knots in this two-inch thread, close to your quilt, and then take three strands of white cotton yarn about two inches long and place over the knot you have just made. Finish your tie by making two more knots with the white thread to secure the yarn in place. Cut your white thread the same length as your yarn.

This same procedure is continued, hit or miss style, over the entire top of your quilt.

Our grandmothers, in many cases when a batting of loose cotton or a wool fleece was used as a filler, would tie the quilts in a widely spaced fashion. When laundering was required the knots were cut, the quilt was then taken apart, the back and top washed and ironed, and the batting put in the sun for a day's airing. The quilt was then retied. Those who do not care for this amount of work should tie the quilt in close range. The batting will hold together through several washings and keep fairly intact.

Many have used cotton blankets for the filler instead of batting. This gives the desired weight and the washings do not disturb the contents inside the quilt.

Tieing may be done with the quilt on the frame as if it were to be quilted. Some tie with the quilting hoop and still others have been known to lay the material on a table and proceed to tie. If done this way, however, the back may not be as taut as if put on a frame and the result may not be satisfactory.

A finished tied quilt.

8. Attach an Edging or Binding

After the coverlet is tied or quilted an edging is added as a finishing touch. The usual procedure is to obtain a 2½-inch-wide strip of material and place it around the entire edge of your quilt, with the right side against the right of your quilt. This edging is usually sewn by machine, about ½ inch from the outside edge of your quilt, then turned over to the back, folded in ¼ inch and then hemmed into place.

If your quilt has a sashing and a separate edging is not desired, make your quilt back larger than the quilt top. Turn this extra material over the top, fold under ¼ inch for the hem and hemstitch into place.

Facts Well Worth Remembering About Quiltmaking

Quilts are made for a number of reasons. Some are made to provide warmth and comfort. Others are made with the idea of using odd bits of material that have accumulated from time to time and need to be put to good use. Still others are made because quilting is a pleasant pastime. But whatever the reason for making a quilt, it must be well made to look good. If you keep these rules in mind, your finished quilt will bring you much joy.

☐ Choose only fast-colored, tightly woven, soft materials.

☐ Sort and grade your materials. Don't mix cottons with wools or silks. Make your quilt with one kind of material.

☐ Study your pattern before actually cutting the material and be sure you have the correct amount of fabric before cutting any design. Many a lovely creation has been ruined by having to supplement a pattern with some off shade in order to complete a quilt. Take account of what you have and adjust your pattern to your needs.

☐ Keep all goods well pressed while cutting and sewing.

☐ Carry out some definite idea throughout the entire quilt.

☐ Be sure the corners miter correctly, edges are even and seams are straight.

☐ Make borders and choose quilt backing to complement the top.

It all sums up this way: to make a worthwhile product you must plan, proceed slowly, choose the correct material and pattern and use the correct needles and thread. With care you can have a quilt that will be the envy of all.

Be exact in cutting, do not hurry with the joining, choose your patterns and colors with care and do not confuse your colors.

Take plenty of time to study your pattern, the colors and the quilting, as well as to take stock of the materials you are to use. The adage "A thing worth doing at all is worth doing well" will serve in good stead here. You want to produce a well-made, attractive, useful heirloom that you, your children, and your grandchildren will be proud to own.

The rules of correct quiltmaking are not hard to follow. They are not confusing. One looks ahead, so to speak, just as one would plan a shopping tour. The path to better quilts is open to all who desire to follow the guide to perfect work.

Patterns

In the following pages you will find fifty patterns, ranging from the simplest straight-line patterns to more complicated arrangements. All yardage instructions are based on a fabric width of 36 inches. The solid line in each pattern is the cut line; the dotted line is the sewing line.

The patterns for borders are only a few suggestions. I'm sure that as you learn this creative handicraft you will develop many of your own.

Broken Sash

This was my first quilt and its simplicity makes it an excellent choice for any beginner. Its beauty lies in its arrangement of strongly contrasting elements. It can be equally effective if the squares are a profusion of different bright colors, with the background triangles all the same neutral shade.

Blocks: 12 inches square

Quilt top: 67½ by 81 inches with sashing and half block border
70½ by 84 inches with sashing and half block plus sashing border
20 full blocks, 18 border half blocks and 4 corner squares

Material you will need
Dark print for A units, sashing (including border) and edging: 4½ yards
Light print for B units: 3½ yards

Each block requires
Dark: 4 unit A
Light: 16 unit B

Finished quilt requires
Dark: 120 unit A
Light: 480 unit B

To make one block
Join four B units to the four sides of an A unit to make a square. Make four of these square sections, and then join them to form the finished block. Press when completed. Make 80

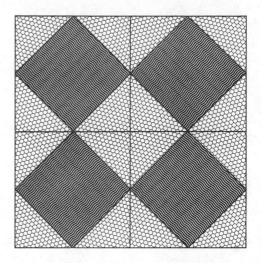

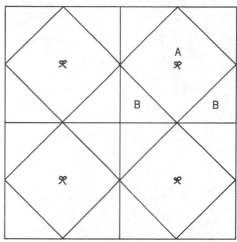

See pages 197 and 198 for color photographs of this quilt.

square sections into 20 full blocks for the quilt top. Make 36 square sections into 18 half blocks for the border and 4 square sections for the corners.

To assemble the quilt top

Make the sashing by making twenty-four strips measuring 2 by 12½ inches, twelve measuring 2 by 6½ inches and five measuring 2 by 81½+ inches. If a sashing is to be used on the border, cut two strips 2 by 70½+ inches and two strips 2 by 84+ inches. A few extra inches added to the length of these long strips is a good idea to allow for possible error. It can always be trimmed off later if not needed. Cutting all of these long strips from the length of the fabric before cutting the A units eliminates the need for piecing them. The narrow edging can be pieced without being too noticeable. Attach the 12½-inch sashing strips to the full blocks to make four strips of five blocks each, adding a half-block to each end. Also make two strips consisting of five half-blocks, six 6½-inch sashing strips and one border square at each end. Lastly join these strips together with the long sashing units to complete the quilt top. After attaching the quilt back and filler, tie the quilt in the centers of the A units and at the intersections of the sashing strips. Sew a 1-inch-wide strip of dark material around the edges of the quilt as a finishing touch.

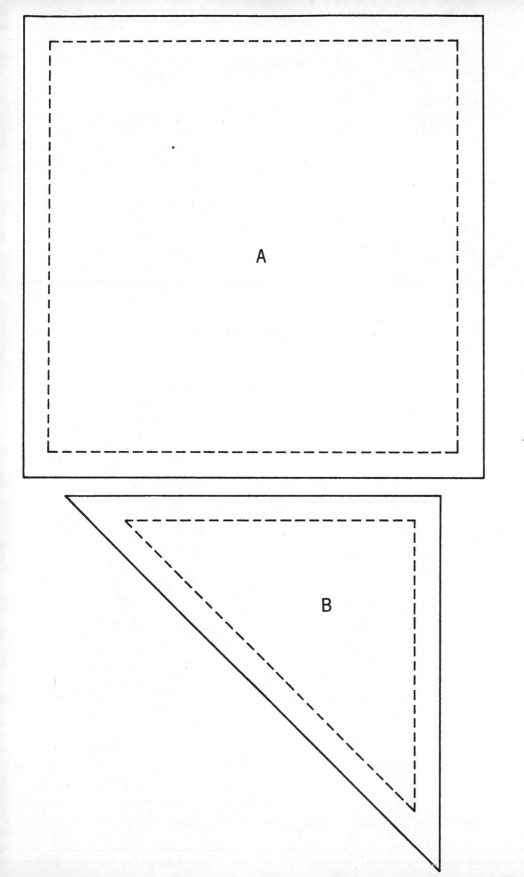

Album Quilt

This pattern has sometimes been named the "Friendship Quilt" because of the presence of friends' names embroidered across the center unit. It is considered one of the oldest patterns known, and many prized heirloom quilts are made from this pattern. In years past this design was used extensively by church women, each one embroidering her name on the block she donated toward the quilt that was sold at the church fair.

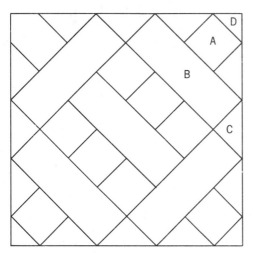

Blocks: 10 inches square

Quilt top: 70 by 90 inches
63 blocks

Material you will need
Print for A and B units: 6 yards
White for A, B, C and D units: 5
   yards

Each block requires
Print: 8 unit A
           4 unit B
White: 2 unit A
           1 unit B
         12 unit C
           4 unit D

Finished quilt top requires
Print: 504 unit A
        252 unit B
White: 126 unit A
         63 unit B
      756 unit C
      252 unit D

To make one block
Make two sections, each consisting of two print A units joined to opposite sides of a white A unit,

and sew these sections to opposite sides of the white B unit to form a square. Make two sections, each having a print B unit with C units at opposite ends. Next make four triangular sections, each one made by attaching two C units to opposite sides of a print A unit and a D unit to a third side. Two of these C-A-D sections are joined to the C-B-C sections to form two large triangles. The remaining two C-A-D sections are joined to the remaining two print B units. These last two sections are then sewn to opposite sides of the square center section. The two large triangles are now sewn to the remaining two sides of the square center section to complete the block. Embroider the name of a friend across the center white unit, and press when completed.

To assemble the quilt top
Blocks may be joined together in straight rows, seven blocks across and nine blocks down. For variation the blocks can be joined diagonally with the edges filled in with large plain triangles. The pieced, autographed blocks can also be joined diagonally, alternating rows of pieced blocks with rows of plain blocks. See illustration.

Blocks: 10 inches square

Quilt top: 70 by 84 inches
30 pieced blocks, 20 plain blocks, 18 large triangles and 4 small triangles

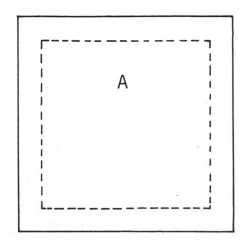

A

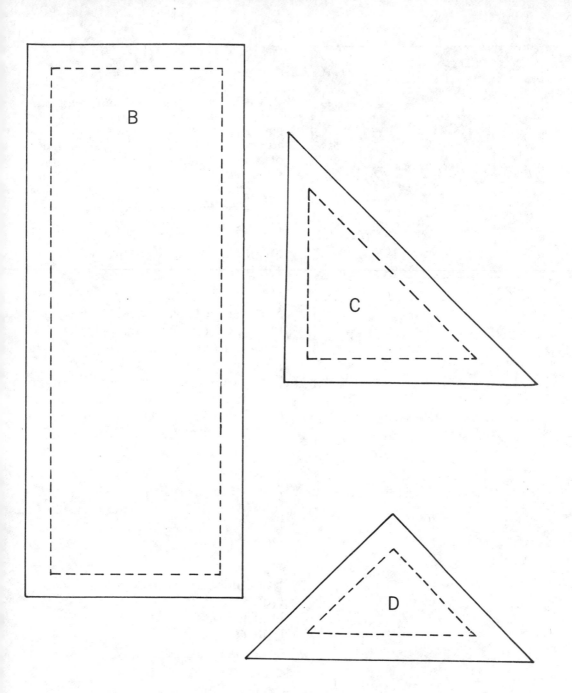

B

C

D

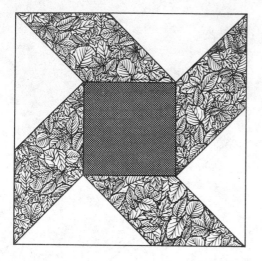

The Open Box

This is an easy straight-seam design. It is ideal for a beginner and interesting enough to hold the attention of the more advanced sewer. Each box is usually made of different colors, making this an odd-scrap design. This design has also been called the Eccentric Star.

Blocks: 7¼ inches square

Quilt top: 72½ by 87 inches
120 blocks

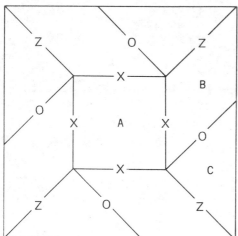

Material you will need
For A units: for each block, 3½-inch square; for entire quilt, 1¼ yards
For B units: for each block, piece 11 by 6½ inches
For C units: for each block, piece 12 by 6 inches; for entire quilt, 3½ yards

Each block requires
Unit A: 1
Unit B: 4
Unit C: 4

Finished quilt requires
Unit A: 120
Unit B: 480
Unit C: 480

To make one block

Make four sections, each consisting of one B unit joined to one C unit. See illustration, seam "O", B-C sections. Press and then join these B-C sections to the four sides of the A unit, seam "X". Then join C unit to adjacent B-C unit at the four corners, seam "Z". Press when completed.

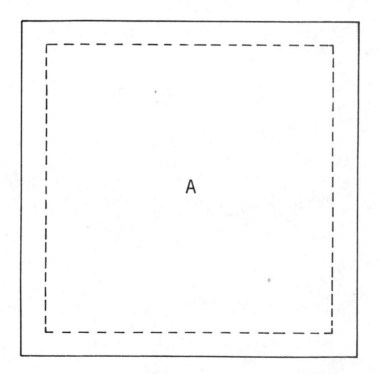

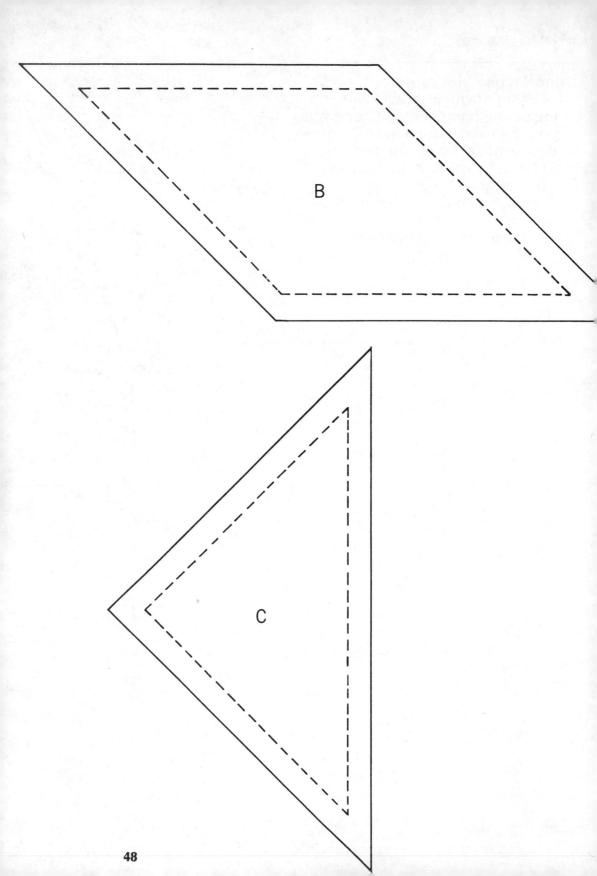

B

C

The Spool

This is a very pleasing design to make and simple for a beginner. Only two cutting patterns are needed. This design may be stitched by machine with ease.

If each spool is made of a different figured print or solid color combined with white or another plain color and joined with a 1½-inch-wide sashing I am sure you will be pleased with the results.

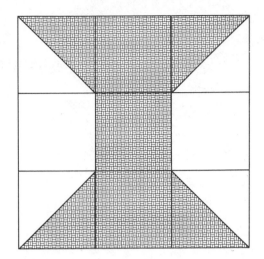

Blocks: 9 inches square

Quilt top: 72 by 90 inches without sashing; 86 by 107 inches with sashing and sashing border
80 blocks

Material you will need
Figured print for A and B units: for
  each block, piece 7½ by 11
  inches
White for A and B units: 4 yards
Sashing: 3 yards

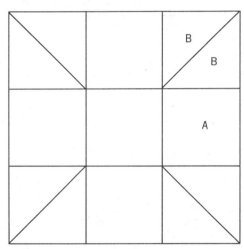

Each block requires
Print: 3 unit A
         4 unit B
White: 2 unit A
         4 unit B

Finished quilt requires
Print: 240 unit A
         320 unit B
White: 160 unit A
         320 unit B

To make one block
Sew white and print B units to-
    gether to form four squares and

press. Join two of these squares to opposite sides of a white A unit, following the diagram. Do this twice, making two rows of three squares each. Then join the three print A units together in a row. After pressing all these sections, join the three rows together. Press when completed.

To cut the sashing

Cut the fabric to be used for sashing first in 2-inch-wide strips the length of the fabric. From these strips you will have nine pieces to be used for the long, lengthwise sashing, two long pieces to be used at the top and bottom edges, and the remainder to cut into 9½-inch pieces to go between the blocks.

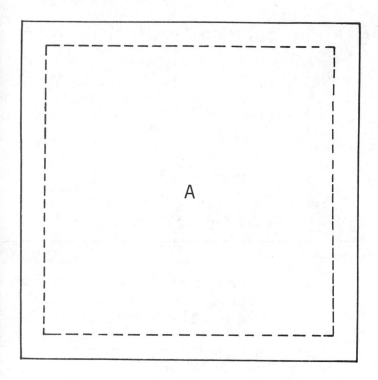

A

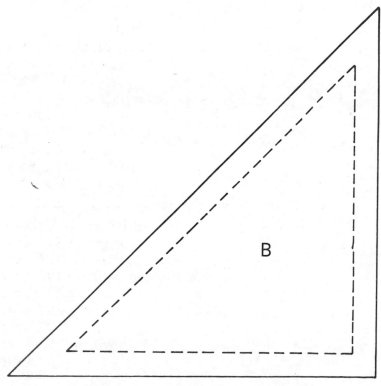

B

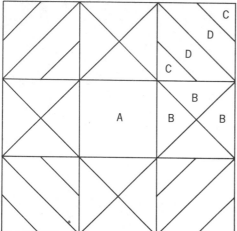

Jackknife Block

This is an attractive, easy-to-piece design that is excellent for beginners.

Gay prints in both light and dark figures give a pleasing effect when combined with a bright orange or yellow and a medium green.

Blocks: 12 inches square

Quilt top: 72 by 96 inches
48 blocks

Material you will need
Green for A and C units: 1½ yards
Light print for B and D units: 3½ yards
Orange for B and D units: 4¾ yards
Dark print for B and C units: 2 yards

Each block requires
Green:	1 unit A
	4 unit C
Light print:	4 unit B
	4 unit D
Orange:	8 unit B
	4 unit D
Dark print:	4 unit B
	4 unit C

Finished quilt requires
Green:	48 unit A
	192 unit C
Light print:	192 unit B
	192 unit D
Orange:	384 unit B
	192 unit D
Dark print:	192 unit B
	192 unit C

To make one block

Make in sections. For the first section, sew the long side of one green C unit to the corresponding side of a dark print D unit. Attach the long side of this unit to the long side of an orange D unit. Attach the opposite side of that unit to the long side of a light print C unit.

For the second section, join a dark print B unit with an orange B unit, sewing the short sides together, to form a large triangle. Repeat using a light print B unit and an orange B unit. Lay these two large triangles together, right sides facing and oranges to prints. Match the center seams and sew the long sides together.

Make four of each section. The result will be eight squares measuring 4½ by 4½ inches to correspond with the center A unit. Sew two of the second sections to opposite sides of the center green A unit. Place the other two second sections between two of the first sections and join. Now sew the three strips together to form the finished block. Press.

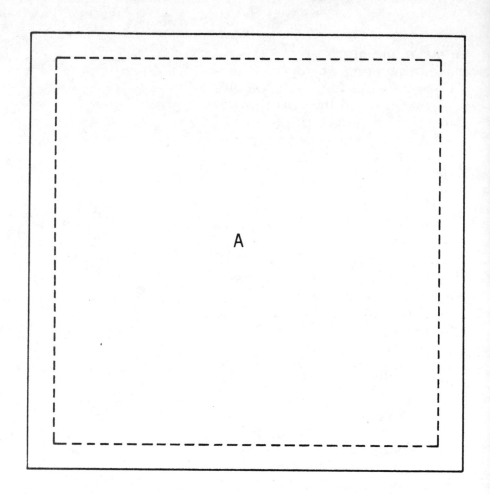

A

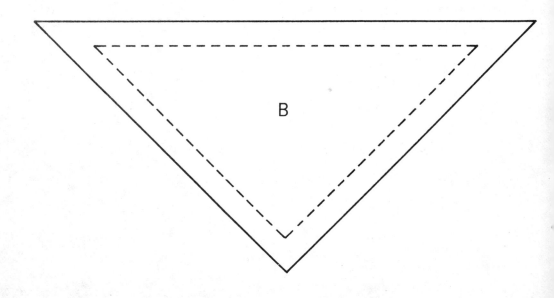

B

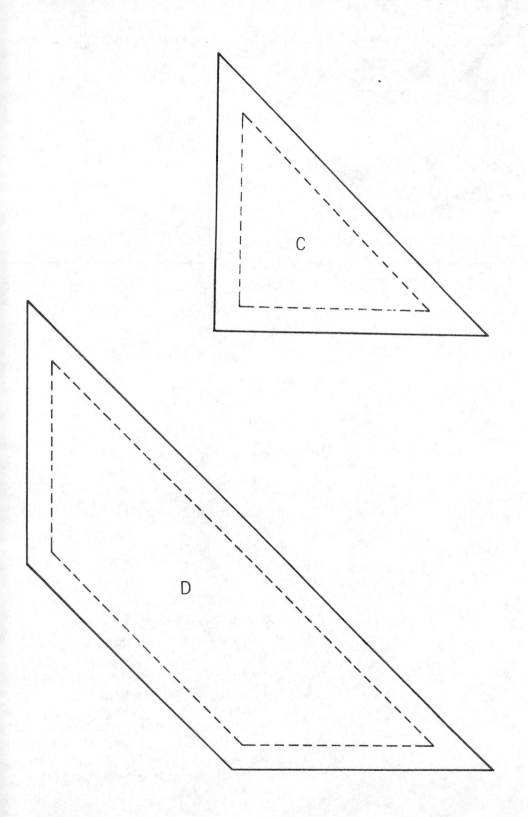

C

D

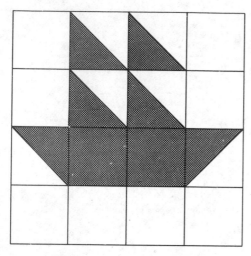

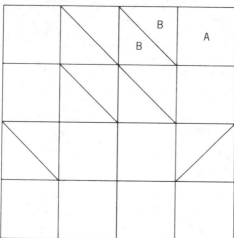

Ship Quilt

Triangles and squares are the only two units needed to make this ship design. Dad and son will both want a quilt like this. If you have limited time this design can be finished very quickly.

Blocks: 12 inches square

Quilt top: 72 by 96 inches
48 blocks

Material you will need
Light (plain or figured) for A and B
    units: 6 yards
Dark (plain or figured) for A and B
    units: 3¼ yards

Each block requires
Light: 8 unit A
         6 unit B
Dark: 2 unit A
        6 unit B

Finished quilt requires
Light: 384 unit A
       288 unit B
Dark: 96 unit A
      288 unit B

To make one block
Begin by piecing all dark and light B units to form six squares. To make the first row (bottom), join four light A units in a row. For the second row, join one pieced section, two dark A units and one pieced section, matching edges according to diagram. Attach this row to first row. Make

the third row by joining one light A unit, two pieced sections and another light A unit, matching edges according to diagram. Connect to preceding row. Make the fourth row exactly as third row and join to third row in the same manner as the third was joined. Press when completed.

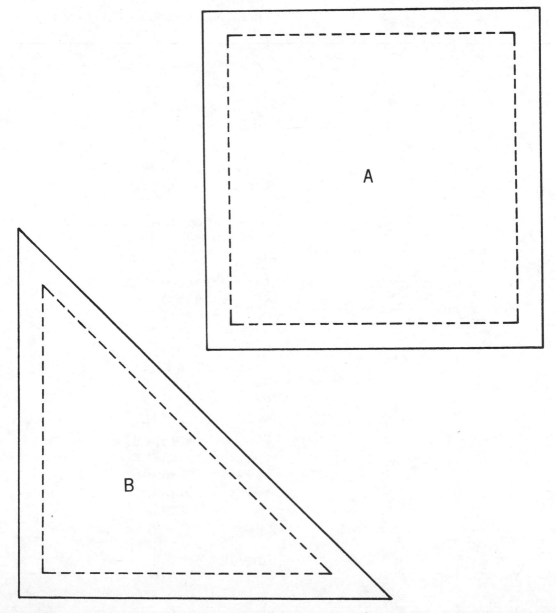

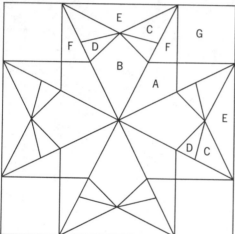

Broken Crystals

Suggestive of a jumbled mass of broken crystal, this newcomer to the quilt world has a definite arrangement of colors that can be fully appreciated only by one who owns a quilt like it. By systematically piecing this block in the suggested sequence, you will have a block that has well-matched points and is worth every bit of effort you have put forth.

Four plain colors seem to carry off this design in the most pleasing manner. Orchid, yellow, medium brown and green are used as an example of maximum beauty.

Blocks: 16 inches square

Quilt top: 80 by 96 inches
30 blocks

Material you will need
Orchid for A and C units: 4½ yards
Yellow for B and F units: 4¾ yards
Green for E and G units: 4 yards
Brown for D units: 1¾ yards

Each block requires
Orchid: 4 unit A
          8 unit C
Yellow: 4 unit B
          8 unit F
Green: 4 unit E
          4 unit G
Brown: 8 unit D

Finished quilt requires
Orchid: 120 unit A
          240 unit C
Yellow: 120 unit B
          240 unit F
Green: 120 unit E
          120 unit G
Brown: 240 unit D

Special cutting note

If the fabric you have chosen for pattern units C, D or F has a right and wrong side, it will be necessary to cut half of the total number of the units facing right and half facing left. This may be easily done by turning the unit pattern upside down for cutting half of the pieces.

To make one block

Follow the Piecing Diagram. Join eight sections containing one C unit and one D unit each (1), four to face right and four to face left. Take care that the shortest side of C unit is matched to the medium length side of D unit. Make four F-A sections; see diagram (2). Make four G-F sections (3). Sew the F-A sections to the G-F sections (4). The result will be four kite-shaped diamonds. Join a right C-D section to the left short side of each B unit (5). Repeat this step three more times. Join the four E units to the C edge of the remaining C-D sections (6). Sew the C-D-B sections to the E-C-D sections (7). The result will be four large triangles. Sew each one of the kite sections to each of the large triangle sections (8). The result will be four sections, each of which is one-quarter of the complete block. Now sew two quarters together to form a half (9). Repeat with the other two quarters. Sew the two halves together (10). The block is now completed. Press.

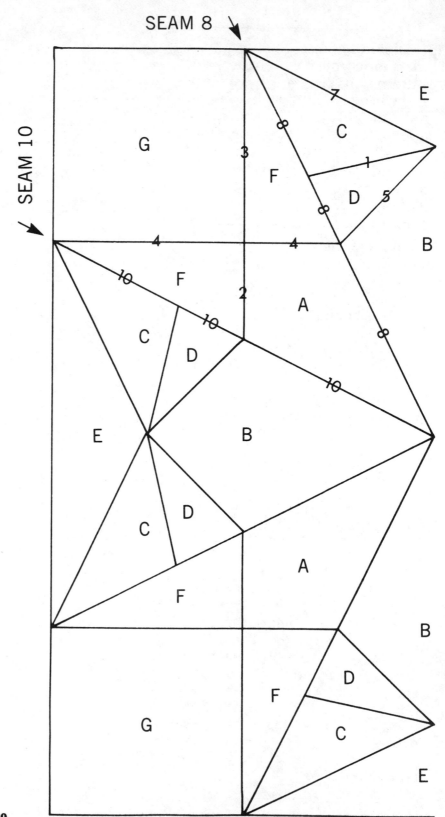

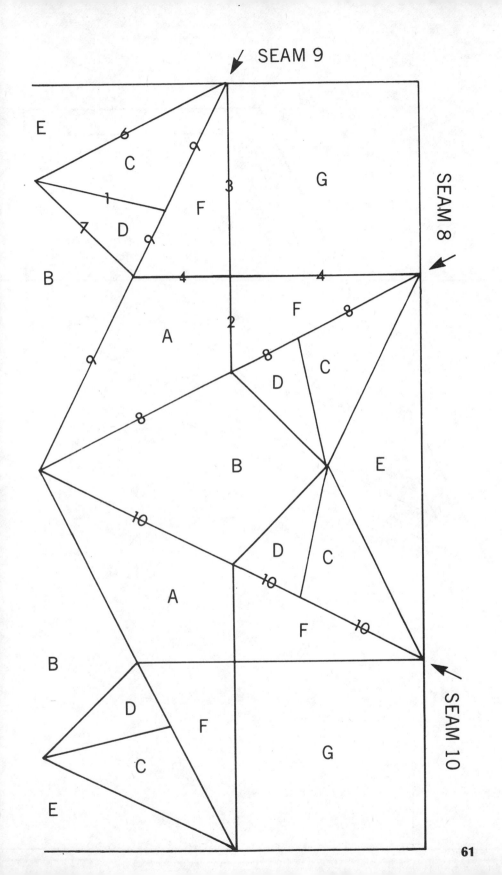

SEAM 9

SEAM 8

SEAM 10

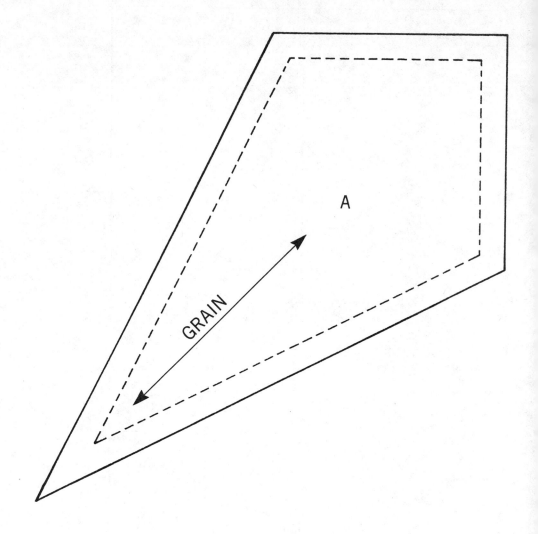

A

GRAIN

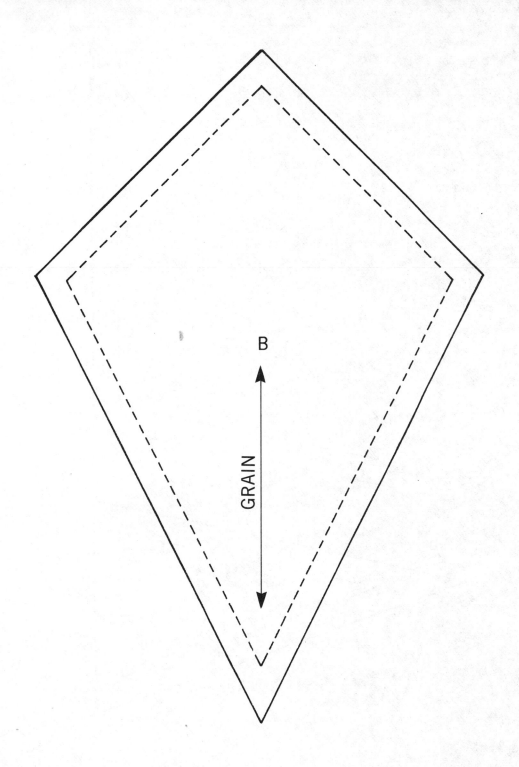

B

GRAIN

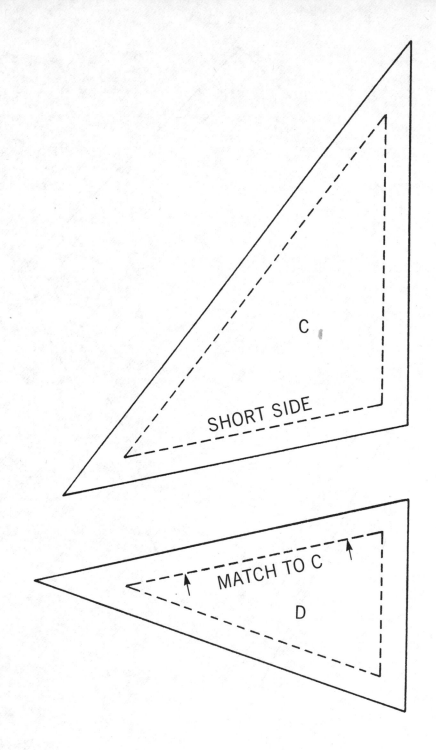

C

SHORT SIDE

MATCH TO C

D

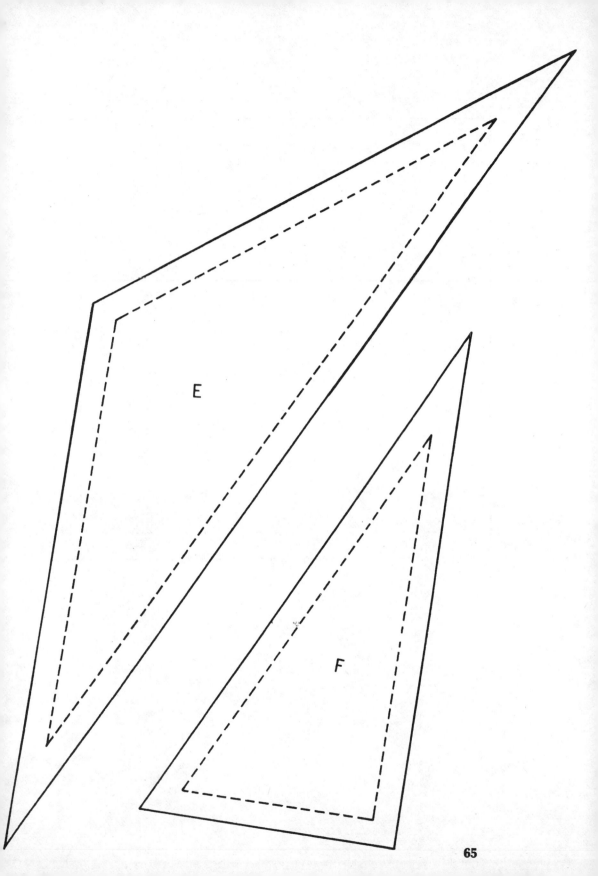

E

F

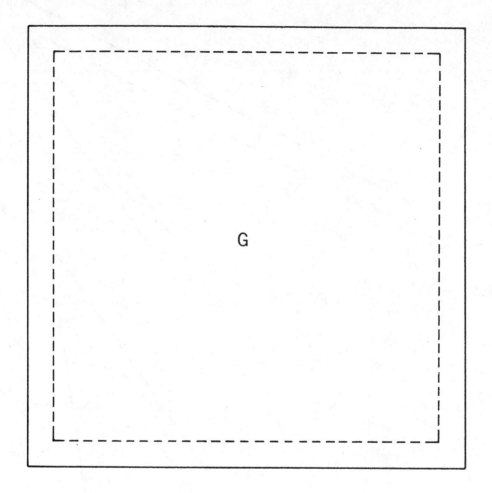

The Airplanes

Are you air minded? This brand-new design will answer the purpose if you are looking for a design for that air-minded son or husband. At any rate it's a delightful pattern and one well worth considering.

A color arrangement that looks pleasing is medium blue for the corner units, a contrasting figured print for the airplane units, combined with white and a red or pink shade.

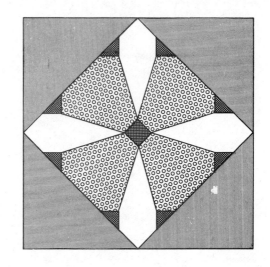

Blocks: 14 inches square

Quilt top: 70 by 98 inches
35 blocks

Material you will need
Red for A and D units: ⅞ yard
Print for B units: 2¾ yards
White for C units: 2¼ yards
Blue for E units: 4¼ yards

Each block requires
Red: 8 unit A
        1 unit D
Print: 4 unit B
White: 4 unit C
Blue: 4 unit E

Finished quilt requires
Red: 280 unit A
         35 unit D
Print: 140 unit B
White: 140 unit C
Blue: 140 unit E

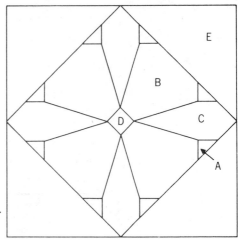

Special cutting note
Use the half E unit pattern to make
a full size pattern before cutting
the fabric. A more accurate piece
can be cut singularly rather than
cutting the fabric folded.

To make one block
Sew two A units to a B unit, making
four such sections. Join two of
these sections to opposite sides
of the D unit. Join two C units to
opposite sides of the remaining
two sections; then join these
two sections to the main section,
first matching the B unit to the D
unit and then the C unit edges to
the A-B sections. Sew the four E
units to this section and press.

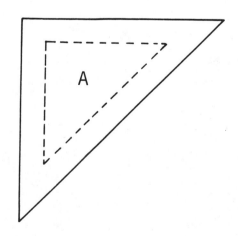

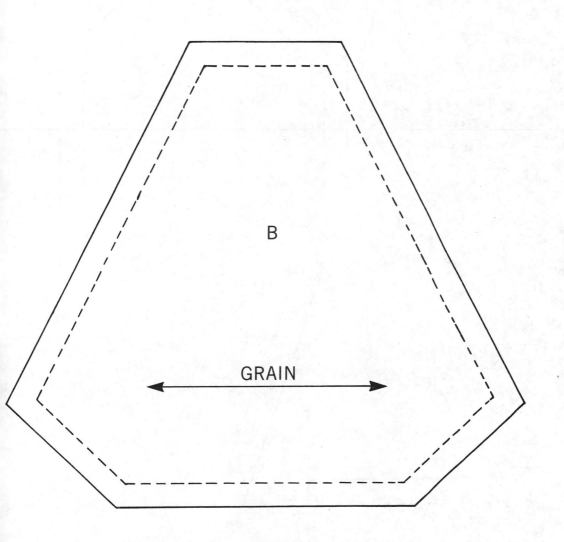

B

GRAIN

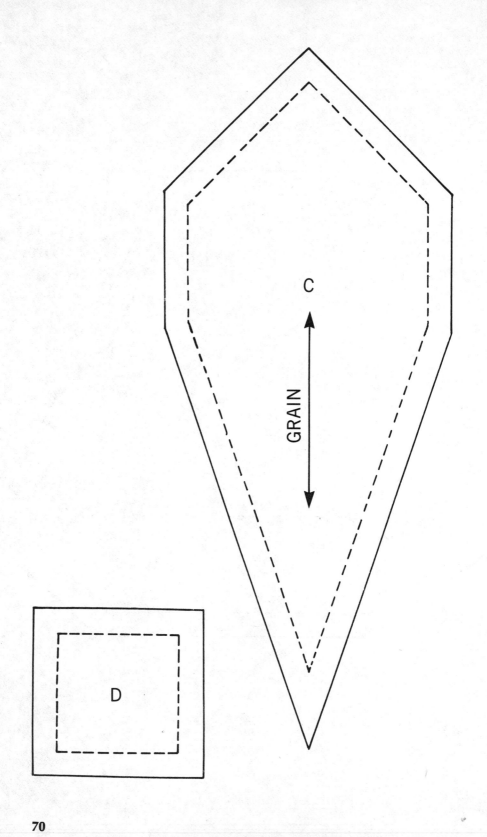

C

GRAIN

D

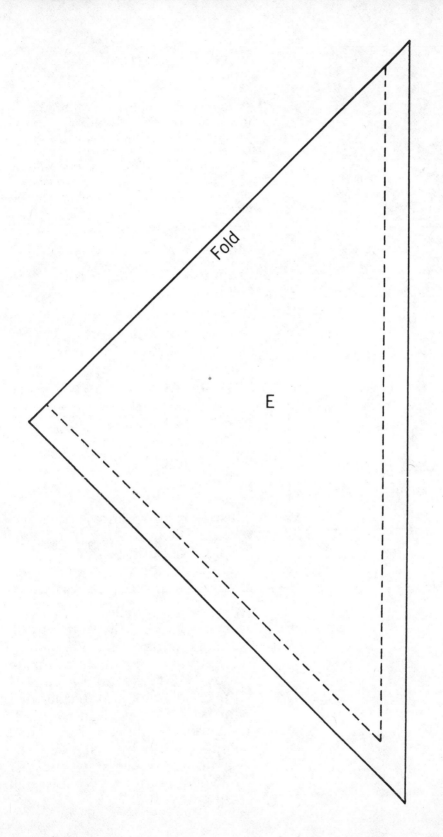

Fold

E

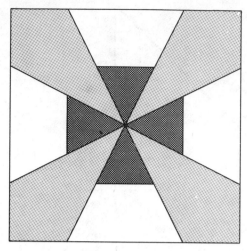

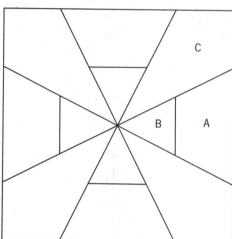

The Pinwheel

A wonderful combination of three colors, this is an all-over pattern that requires no sashing. In the event a sashing is desired, fewer blocks are needed and you can individualize each block by using a different color for each one. Use any two shades of one color, figured or plain, and plain white.

Blocks: 8 inches square

Quilt top: 72 by 96 inches
108 blocks

Material you will need
White for A units: 3¾ yards
Purple for B units: 2¼ yards
Orchid for C units: 6¼ yards

Each block requires
White: 4 unit A
Purple: 4 unit B
Orchid: 4 unit C

Finished quilt requires
White: 432 unit A
Purple: 432 unit B
Orchid: 432 unit C

To make one block
Join all A and B units to form triangular sections. Press. Attach a C unit to each A-B section, making four A-B-C sections. Each of these sections is one-quarter of the whole block. Join two A-B-C sections, making a half block. Repeat with the last two A-B-C sections. Now sew the two halves together to complete the full block. Press.

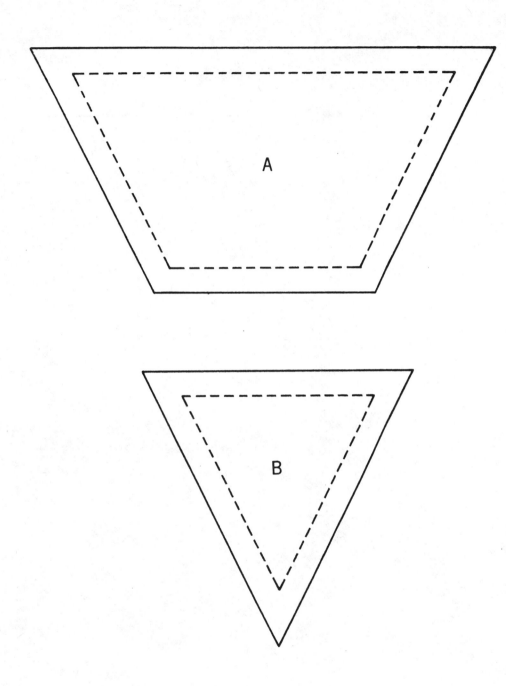

A

B

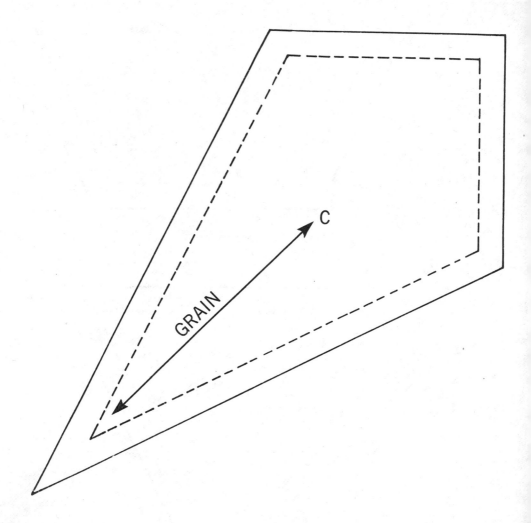

C

GRAIN

Century of Progress

This design is a revelation to say the least. It is a brand-new pattern and one that is bound to be a favorite wherever it is seen. The seams are relatively simple, making it a good pattern that challenges the beginner without being impossible.

Bright colors run riot in this design. You could use bright pink, medium blue and a small, figured print of the same gay colors. You will have color, beauty and charm.

Blocks: 13 inches square

Quilt top: 78 by 91 inches
42 blocks

Material you will need
Pink for A, F and G units: 4 yards
Blue for B and D units: 2¼ yards
Print for C, E and G units: 4 yards

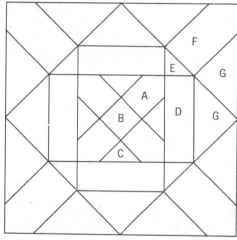

Each block requires
Pink: 4 unit A
       4 unit F
       4 unit G
Blue: 1 unit B
       4 unit D
Print: 4 unit C
       4 unit E
       8 unit G

Finished quilt requires
Pink: 168 unit A
      168 unit F
      168 unit G
Blue: 42 unit B
      168 unit D
Print: 168 unit C
      168 unit E
      336 unit G

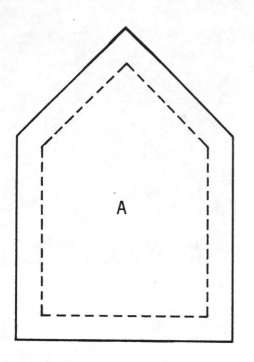

A

To make one block
Join the C units to the long sides of two A units, making two triangular sections. Attach the two remaining A units to opposite sides of the B unit. Place this section between the other two and join to form a square. Sew two D units to opposite sides of this square. Now attach the E units to opposite ends of the two remaining D units and join to the main section. Attach one pink G unit to each remaining free side of a D unit, forming a larger square. Now make four triangular sections by sewing two print G units to each F unit. Join these sections to the main square to make the finished square. Press when completed.

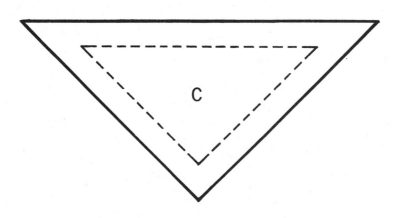

C

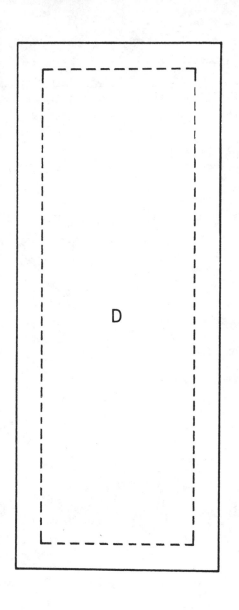

D

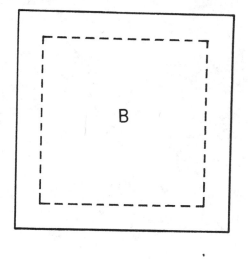

B

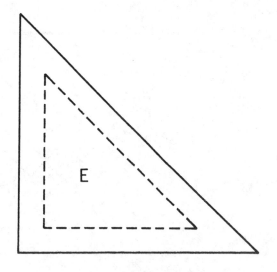

E

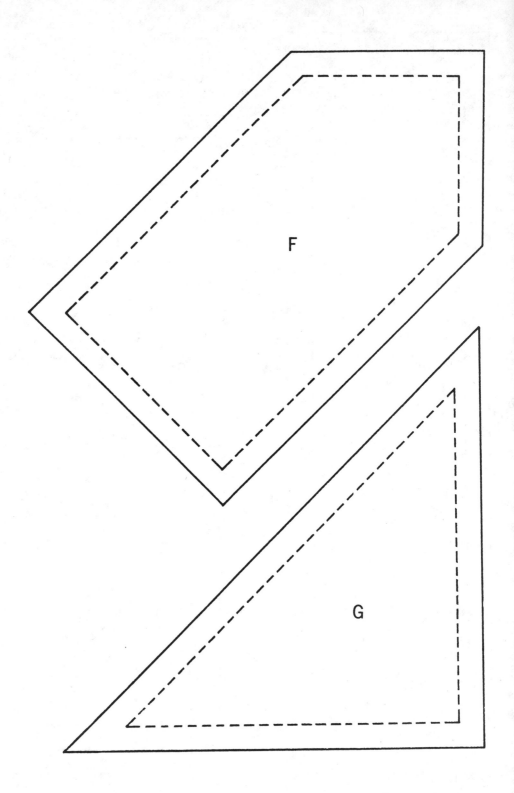

F

G

The Maple Leaf

Just the thing for shades of green, red, gold, rust and yellow. Every leaf unit can have a new combination of colors. No pattern could be more delightful to work with, and surely few could be easier to make.

This leaf, like other patterns in the old-time design, should be joined to alternating plain squares.

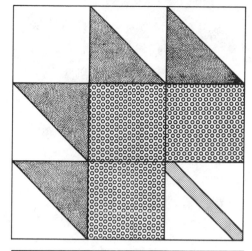

Blocks: 9 inches square

Quilt top: 81 by 99 inches
50 pieced blocks and 40 plain blocks

Material you will need
Print for A units: for each block, piece 3½ by 10½ inches or 7 inches square
Plain color for B units: for each block, piece 3½ by 7 inches
White for A and B units: 2½ yards
Green for C units: ¼ yard
Plain color for alternating plain squares: 4½ yards

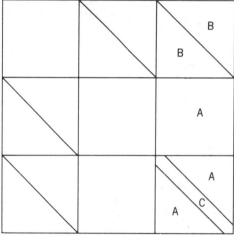

Each block requires
Print: 3 unit A
Plain: 4 unit B
White: 2 unit A
         4 unit B
Green: 1 unit C

Finished quilt requires
Print: 150 unit A
Plain: 200 unit B
White: 100 unit A
         200 unit B
Green: 50 unit C
Plain: 49 blocks   9½ inches
         square

To make one block

Appliqué the C unit to a white A unit, turning under only the long edges. The raw edge on the ends will be caught as the rest of the block is sewn together. Join this section to the three figured A units to form a square. Make four more squares, using for each one a plain and a white B unit. Following the diagram, join two of these squares together and then the other two, making two sections of two squares each. Join one of these sections to the large square section. Attach a white A unit to the plain-colored end of the other two-square section and join this to the main section to form the finished block.

An alternate method is to make four square sections using one plain and one white B unit for each. Following the diagram, join one B-B section to a print A unit and then the C-A section to the B-B-A section. This makes the bottom row. Continue to follow the diagram and sew together a B-B section and two print A units, the middle row, and then the white A unit to the remaining B-B sections. Sew these three rows together to complete the block.

After making all pieced blocks join them to the plain blocks, alternating the pieced and plain blocks. Press when completed.

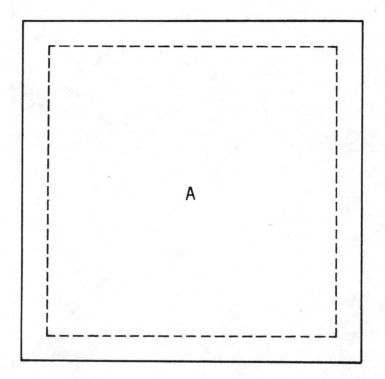

A

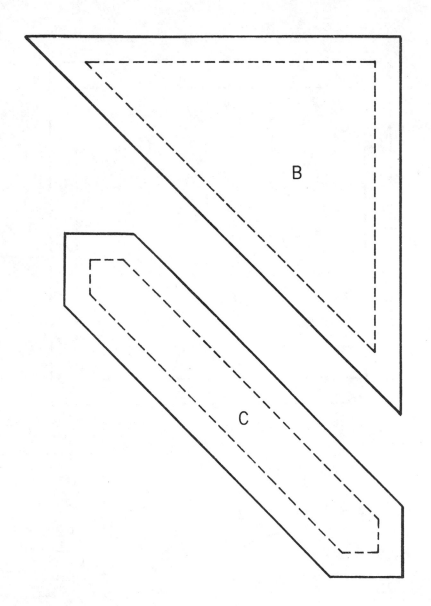

B

C

Abe Lincoln's Platform

In 1860 after a number of debates between Abe Lincoln and Stephen Douglas, a busy housewife from Illinois designed and dedicated this pattern to "Honest Abe." Thus we take our hats off to the thrifty women of Illinois for this inspiring pattern.

Blocks: 14 inches square

Quilt top: 70 by 98 inches
35 blocks

Material you will need
Plain blue for A and C units: 1¾ yards
Red print for B units: ⅞ yard
Striped blue and white for D units: 1⅝ yards
White for E and F units: 3¼ yards
Plain red for F units: 2¼ yards

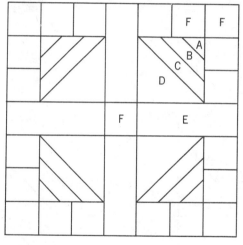

Each block requires
Blue:	4 unit A
	4 unit C
Print:	4 unit B
Striped:	4 unit D
White:	4 unit E
	8 unit F
Red:	13 unit F

Finished quilt top requires
Blue:	140 unit A
	140 unit C
Print:	140 unit B
Striped:	140 unit D
White:	140 unit E
	280 unit F
Red:	455 unit F

Special cutting note

When cutting the D units from striped fabric, make sure that stripes are perpendicular to the longest side of the triangle and that the same color stripe is centered at the opposite angle, the right angle, on each piece cut.

To make one block

Join an A unit to a B unit, then add on a C unit. Next join this piece to a D unit to form a square; make four of these sections. Now piece together a red and white F unit and

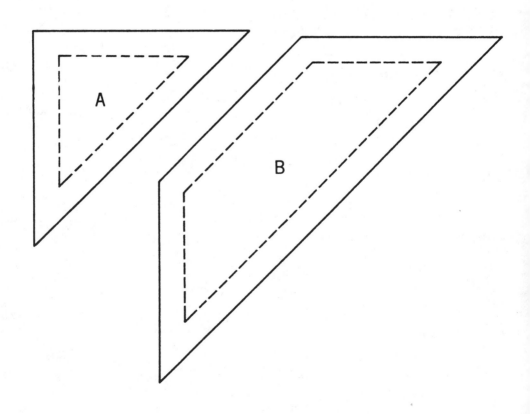

join to the first section made. This forms a rectangle. Make four of these sections. Now join two red and one white F units. Make four of these sections. Join these F-F-F sections to the previously made rectangles, making four larger squares. Join two of these sections together with an E unit in the center; repeat once. The two remaining E units are then joined together with a red F unit in the center. The two main sections are attached to either side of the last section, making a 14-inch square. Press when completed.

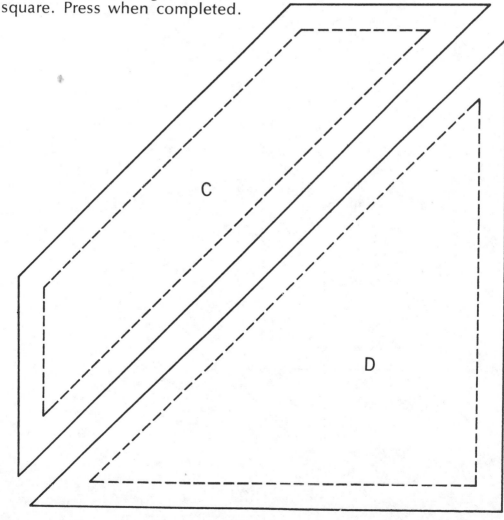

C

D

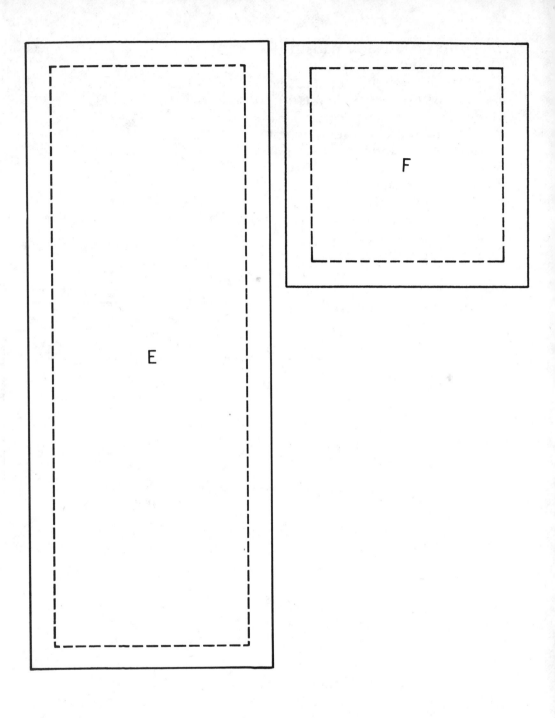

Six-Pointed Star

This design looks complicated but if you follow a few basic rules you'll find it simple and pleasing. The stars are made of twelve triangles, six of a solid color and six of a print. These elements should be different from star to star, but the same solid color and the same print should be used throughout one star. The stars are stitched into white squares, or they may be pieced to complete the block as shown here. These star blocks are joined alternately with squares of a dark solid to complete the quilt top.

Blocks: 5½ inches square

Quilt top: 71½ by 82½ inches, without border
77½ by 88½ inches, with border as shown in the photograph
195 blocks: 98 pieced and 97 plain

Material you will need
Print for A units: piece 9 by 2 inches for each block
Solid for A units: piece 9 by 2 inches for each block
White for B and C units or 6-inch squares to appliqué and border: 4 yards
Solid color for alternating squares and border: 3½ yards

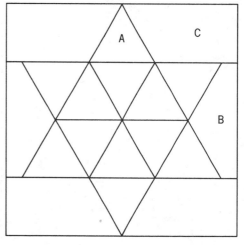

See pages 195 and 196 for color photographs of this quilt.

Each block requires
Print: 6 unit A
Solid: 6 unit A
White: 2 unit B
         4 unit C
         or one 6-inch square

Finished quilt requires

Print: 588 unit A
Solid: 588 unit A
White: 196 unit B
         392 unit C
         or 98 6-inch squares
Solid: 97 6-inch squares
White border: 2-inch-wide strips:
   two pieces 2 by 75+ inches
   two pieces 2 by 86+ inches
Solid border: 2-inch-wide strips:
   two pieces 2 by 79+ inches
   two pieces 2 by 90+ inches

To make one block — all pieced

Make one row of the star by piecing together three print and two solid A units. Next make another row of three solid and two print A units, and join these two rows together. Add a B unit to each side of this section. Now join the C units to the two remaining A units and attach these two sections to the main section to form the finished block.

To make one block — appliquéd

Make one row of the star by piecing together three print and two solid A units. Next, make another row of three solid and two print A units. Join these two rows together as in the illustration. Now, join the remaining A units to the center triangles of the previously joined rows, print A unit to solid A unit. Turn under the ¼-inch seam allowance all the way around this star and baste onto the white 6-inch blocks. To line up the star straight on the block, mark the center of two opposite sides and place opposite points ¼ inch in from the cut edges at the center marks. These points are the top and bottom of the block. The four remaining points will fall into place approximately ¾ inch from the cut edges. Blind stitch the star into place, remove the basting stitches, and press the completed block.

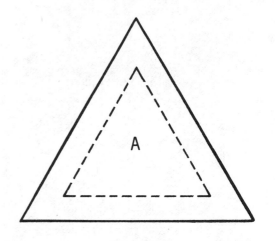

To assemble the quilt top

Join the blocks together, alternating pieced and plain blocks. The quilt top should be thirteen blocks wide and fifteen blocks long. Now add the white border strips and then the border strips of the same material used for the plain squares. Miter the corners. After attaching the filler and quilt back, finish the edge with a narrow strip of white bias tape or fabric. An especially attractive effect can be created by doing the quilting in interesting patterns. You can quilt the plain blocks in a circle design, use diamond shapes for the borders, and squares for the white background in the pieced blocks.

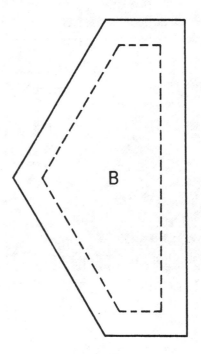

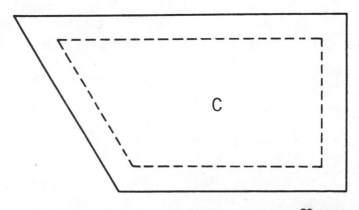

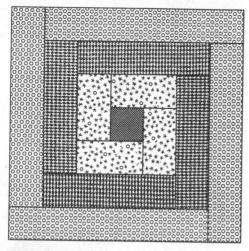

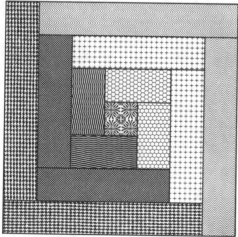

Log Cabin

Here are two of the many ways to assemble the long-famous Log Cabin pattern, one of the older patchwork designs known to the quilt world. The name itself brings to mind a picture of the homes of the earliest American settlers. Each row in this odd-scrap design can be a different figured or plain material, with a red center unit signifying the chimney in the log cabins of long ago. Alternatively, a different effect may be created by using all dark prints for the left and light prints for the right. Other variations can be made by rearrangement of light and dark units and different directions in which the blocks are assembled to form the top.

Blocks: 17½ inches square

Quilt top: 70 by 87½ inches
20 blocks

Material you will need for each block

Red or dark print for A unit: 3-inch
    square
Print #1 for B units: one piece 12
    by 5½ inches, or two pieces each
    6 by 5½ inches, one dark print
    and one light
Print #2 for C units: one piece 12
    by 10½ inches or two contrasting
    pieces 6 by 10½ inches
Print #3 for D units: one piece 12
    by 15½ inches or two contrasting
    pieces 6 by 15½ inches

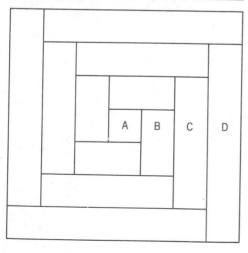

Each block requires
Red or dark print: 1 unit A

AND

Print #1: 4 unit B
Print #2: 4 unit C
Print #3: 4 unit D

OR

Dark #1: 2 unit B
    #2: 2 unit C
    #3: 2 unit D
Light #1: 2 unit B
    #2: 2 unit C
    #3: 2 unit D

Special cutting note
Use the half patterns for units C and D to make full size patterns before cutting the fabric. More accurate pieces can be cut singularly rather than by cutting the fabric folded.

To assemble one block
Being careful to follow the design you have chosen, join the four B units to the sides of the center A unit. Then attach the four C units and finally the four D units. Press when completed.

To assemble the quilt top
After all the blocks have been completed, lay all of them out (four across and five down). Move them around to find a pleasing balance of colors and light and dark corners. When you have found the best arrangement, number the blocks so that it will be easy to join them in the correct order.

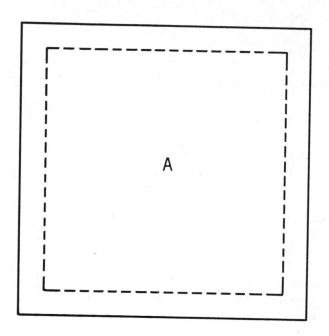

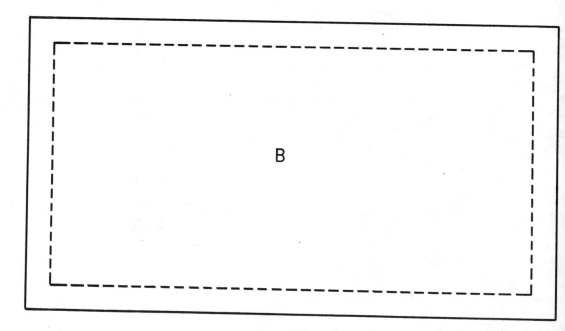

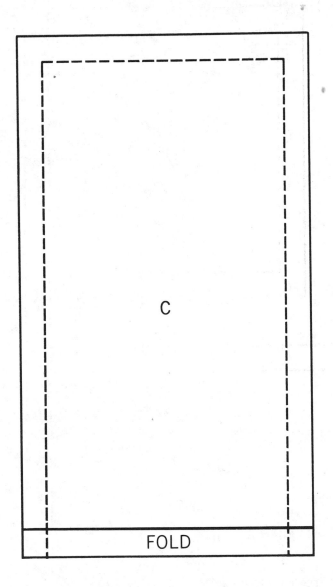

C

FOLD

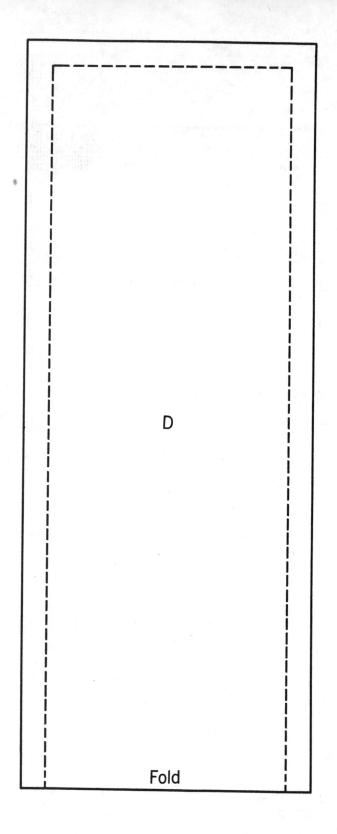

D

Fold

Roman Stripe

This is an ideal pattern for using up scrap pieces, and is simple yet interesting to do. It is a very good pattern for a beginner. It is easy to cut because there is only one pattern and is easy to sew because of the minimum number of corners to be concerned about matching. The same solid color should be used in the center of each three-piece unit. Your quilt will then look unified no matter how many different prints and patterns are used throughout.

Blocks: 9 inches square

Quilt top: 72 by 90 inches
80 blocks

Material you will need
Yellow or other solid for center
  stripes: 2¾ yards
Assorted prints: piece 2 by 5 inches for each stripe

Each block requires
Yellow: 4 units
Prints: 8 units

Finished quilt requires
Yellow: 320 units
Prints: 640 units

To make one block
Attach two print units to the sides of a yellow unit. Make four such sections and then join them according to the diagram.

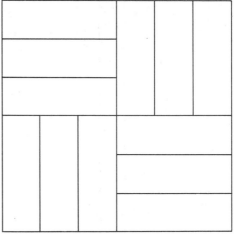

See pages 107 and 108 for color photographs of this quilt.

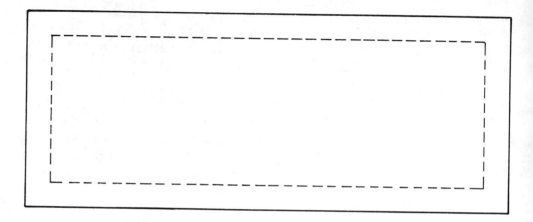

Grand Right and Left

We know that this pattern must have originated back in the days of old square dances, for it surely keeps pace with the jig time of country hoedowns. It will make up quickly and is a charming reminder of the "Old Days" when our grandmothers not only danced to the "Grand Right and Left" but also knew how to make a coverlet that was as graceful and charming as a dance well performed.

Blocks: 16 inches square

Quilt top: 80 by 96 inches
30 blocks

Material you will need
Green or other solid for A units: 4 yards
Orchid or other solid for B and C units: 4¼ yards
Figured print for B and C units: 2½ yards

Each block requires
Green: 4 unit A
Orchid: 4 unit B
               32 unit C
Print: 4 unit B
               16 unit C

Finished quilt top requires
Green: 120 unit A
Orchid: 120 unit B
               960 unit C
Print: 120 unit B
               480 unit C

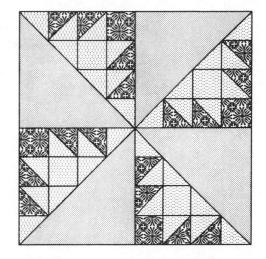

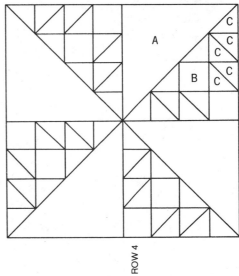

ROW 4

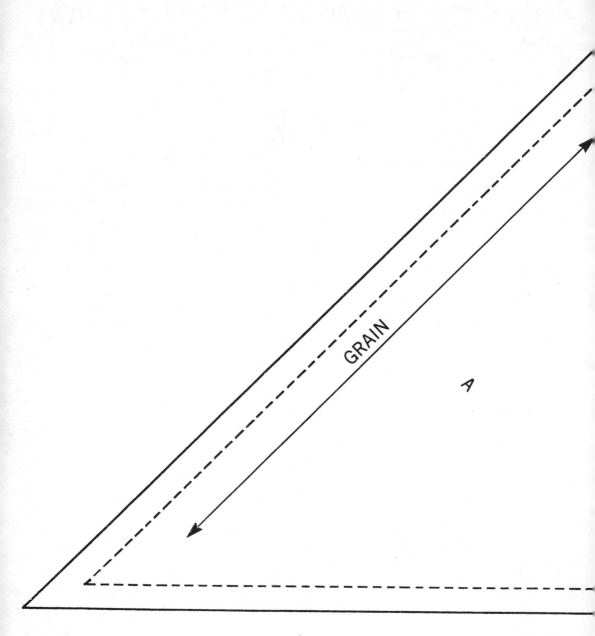

GRAIN

A

Special cutting note
Use the half A unit pattern to make a full-size pattern before cutting the fabric. A more accurate piece can be cut singularly rather than cutting the fabric folded.

To make one block
Make a triangle as follows: Row 1: Join together three orchid C units, two print C units and one print B unit according to the diagram. Row 2: two orchid C units, one orchid B unit and one print C unit. Row 3: two orchid C units and one print C unit. Row 4: one orchid C unit. Make these four rows and join them together. (See notes in the book on the diagram.) *Be careful to follow the pattern correctly,* and then join this triangle to an A unit. Make three more of these squares and then piece them together to form the completed block. Press.

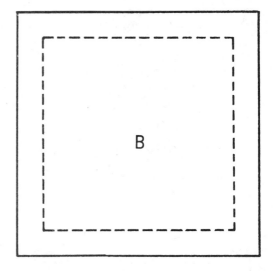

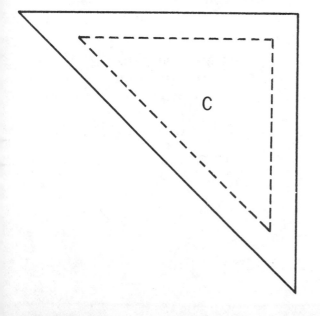

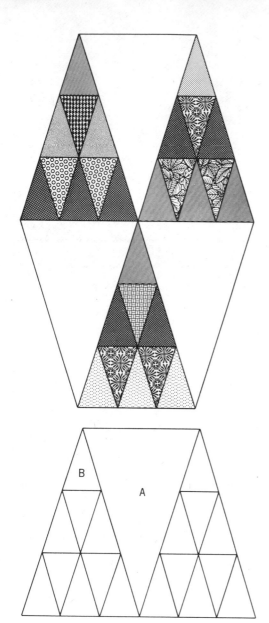

See pages 107 and 108 for color photographs
of this quilt.

The Pyramid

Solid color triangles alternating with pieced triangles of gay prints create colorful interest in this beautiful quilt. Its simple, straight-line construction makes it a good quilt for women new at quiltmaking, while the variation in the colored triangles holds the interest of even the most experienced quilter. The greater the variety of solid and print scraps for the small triangles, the greater the color interest.

Triangles: 3 by 5 by 5 inches

Quilt top: 63 inches at the narrowest point and 66 inches at the widest point of the width by 81 inches long
774 triangles

Material you will need
White or other solid for A units: 4 yards
Solid and print scraps for B units: piece 1¾ by 2¾ inches

Each triangle requires
1 unit A or
9 unit B

Finished quilt requires
387 plain triangles, unit A
387 pieced triangles, 3483 unit B pieces

To make a pieced triangle

Make three rows. The first row consists of one solid B unit. For the second row, attach two solid B units of another shade to a print B unit. Make the third row by alternating five B units, three of another solid color and two of another print or two different prints. Join the three rows and press.

To assemble the quilt top

Make nine strips of 43 triangles each, 22 pieced and 21 plain, starting with a pieced triangle pointing up and alternating with a plain triangle pointing down. End with a pieced triangle. This strip will be as long as the widest point of the finished quilt top. Now make nine strips of 43 triangles each, 22 plain and 21 pieced, starting with a plain triangle pointing down and alternating with a pieced triangle pointing up. End with a plain triangle. Join one each of these two different strips, matching plain to pieced triangles as in the diagram. Repeat this procedure to form nine double strips of triangles. Then join these double strips together to form the quilt top. The resulting scalloped edge may be left as is for a pleasing look over the edge of the bed, or the scallops can be filled in with half triangles.

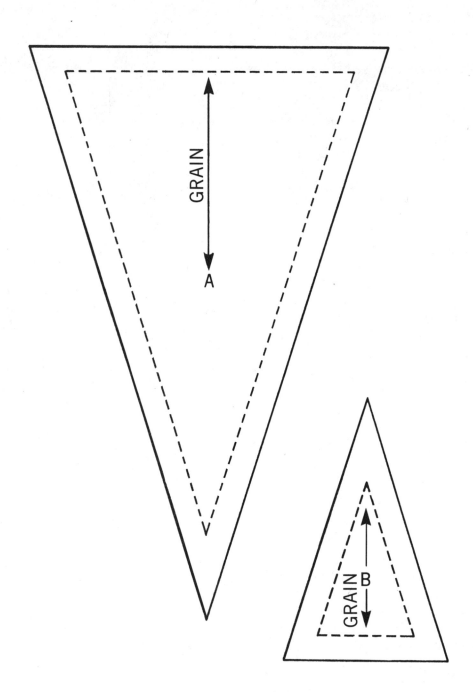

Jack's Blocks

A figured print and a contrasting plain color make this design interesting, attractive and a joy to own. The large blocks are not difficult to assemble, and as only twenty blocks are needed to make an average-sized quilt, this design will make up quickly.

Blocks: 18 inches square

Quilt top: 72 by 90 inches
20 blocks

Material you will need
Figured print for A units: 3 yards
Green or other solid for B units: 2 yards
White for C units: 3¼ yards

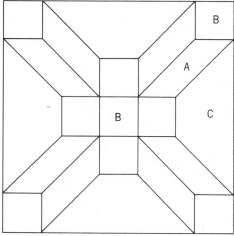

Each block requires
Print: 8 unit A (cut 4 facing left and 4 facing right)
Green: 9 unit B
White: 4 unit C

Finished quilt top requires
Print: 160 unit A (80 facing left and 80 facing right)
Green: 180 unit B
White: 80 unit C

Special cutting note
To cut half of the A units facing left and half facing right, either make two patterns and mark one left and the other right or after cutting half of the pieces turn the pattern upside down to cut the remaining half.

Use the half C unit pattern to make a full size pattern before cutting the fabric. A more accurate piece can be cut singularly rather than cutting the fabric folded.

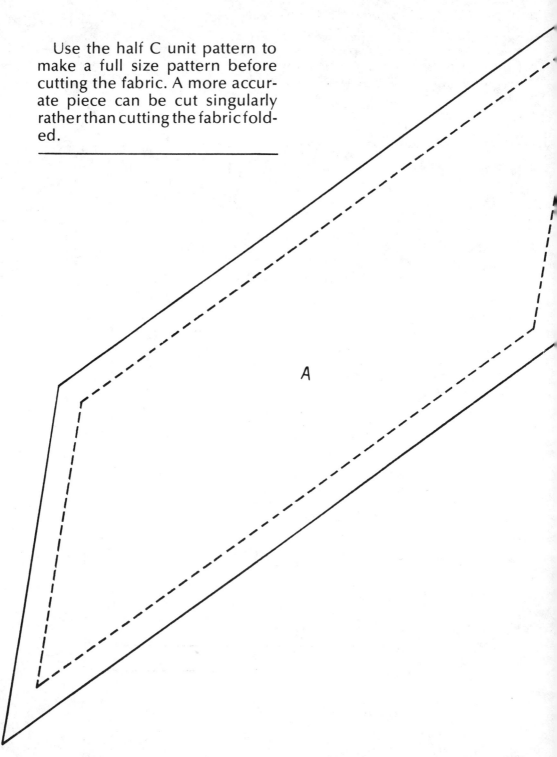

A

To make one block

Join a left A and a right A unit and add a B unit to the end to form the corner of the block; make four such sections. Now make four more sections by joining a B unit to the shortest side of each C unit. Press all sections made. Now attach two of the A-B sections to the sides of a B-C section; make two such sections. The two remaining C-B sections are joined to opposite sides of the remaining B unit. Finally join the two large sections to the sides of the last section made, thus making an 18-inch block. Press.

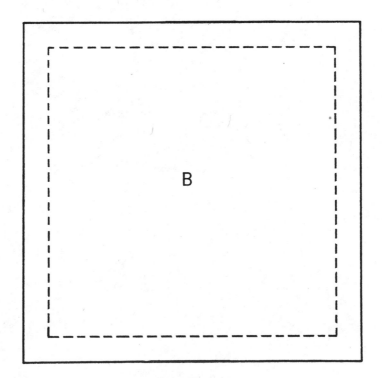

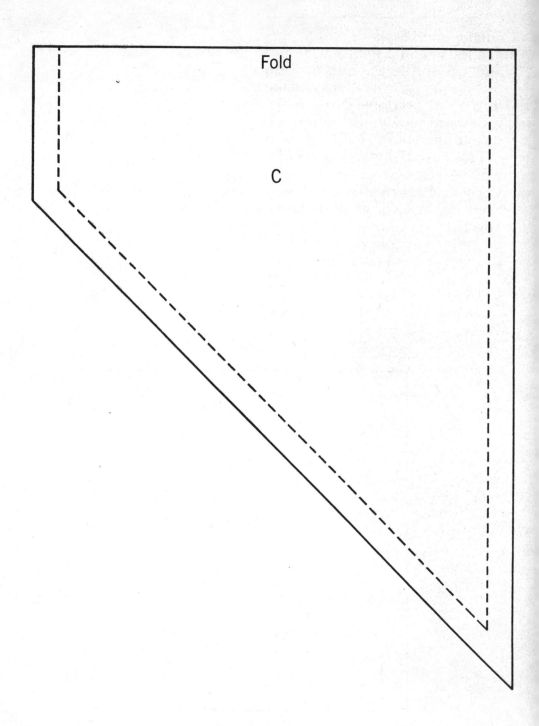

Fold

C

Opposite: The Pyramid (left) and Roman Stripe (right)

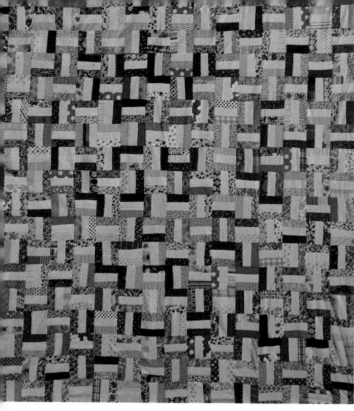

Roman Stripe
(Pattern on page 95)

The Pyramid
(Pattern on page 99)

Opposite: The Necktie and
Eight-Pointed Star

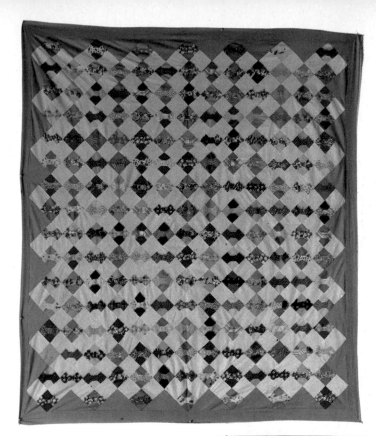

The Necktie
(Pattern on page 140)

Eight-Pointed Star
(Pattern on page 130)

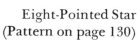

Opposite:
Mohawk Trail variation
and Dresden Plate

Dresden Plate
(Pattern on page 186)

Below: Detail of
Dresden Plate, showing
finishing of back corner

Dresden Plate variation,
with sashing

Opposite: Mohawk Trail

Mohawk Trail
(Pattern on page 168)

Mohawk Trail variation

The Rainbow Square

Entirely new to the quilt world, this pattern is alive and pulsating with charm and beauty as lovely as the pot-o'-gold at the rainbow's end. Anyone who is lucky enough to own such a quilt should be rightly proud of her possession.

Blocks: 18 inches square

Quilt top: 72 by 90 inches
20 blocks

Material you will need
Pink for A and C units: 1¼ yards
White for B and E units: 2 yards
Yellow for D and F units: 2¾ yards
Lavender for E units: 2¼ yards

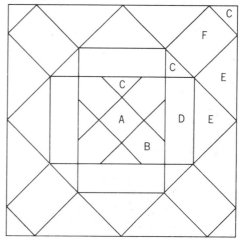

Each block requires
Pink: 1 unit A
              12 unit C
White: 4 unit B
               4 unit E
Yellow: 4 unit D
               4 unit F
Lavender: 8 unit E

Finished quilt requires
Pink: 20 unit A
             240 unit C
White: 80 unit B
              80 unit E
Yellow: 80 unit D
              80 unit F
Lavender: 160 unit E

To make one block

Join two B units to opposite sides of the A unit. Join C units to opposite straight sides of two remaining B units and then attach these two sections to opposite sides of the first section, making a square. Now sew two D units to opposite sides of this square; attach a C unit to each end of the two remaining D units and join these to the other two sides of the center square. Join white E units to the D units forming a larger square. Now attach a C unit to a short side of an F unit and sew a lavender E unit to each long side, forming a triangle. Make four of these sections and join them to the four sides of the large square. This forms an even larger square and completes the block. Press.

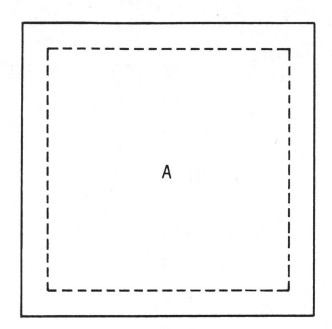

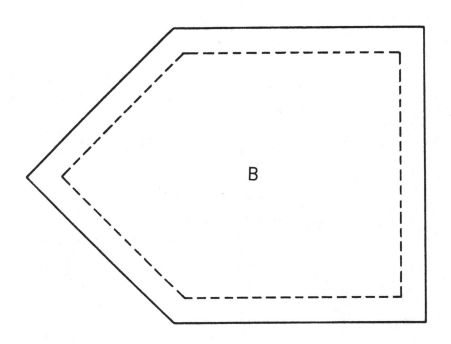

117

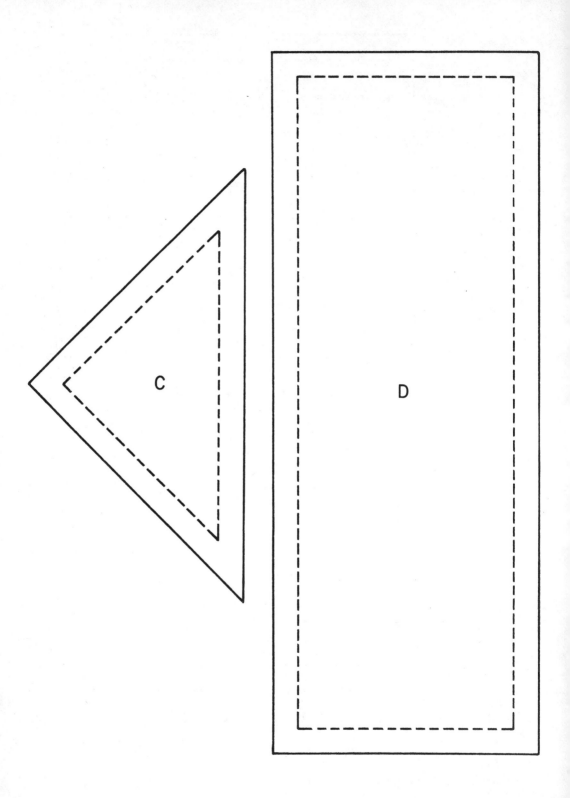

C

D

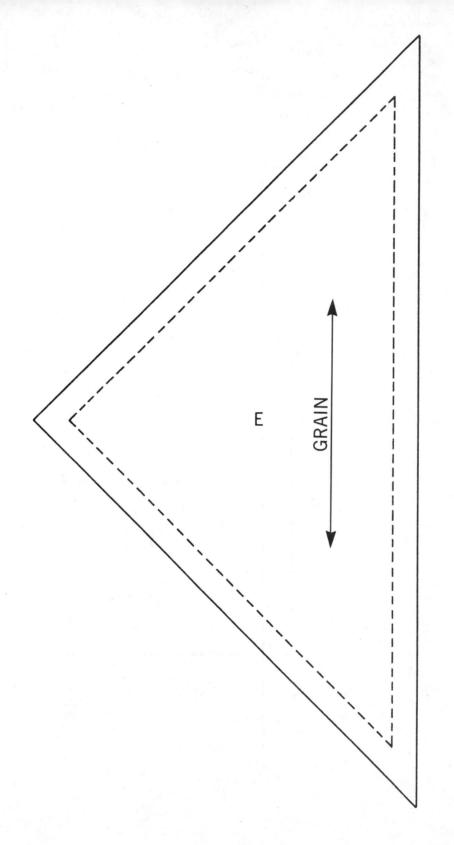

E

GRAIN

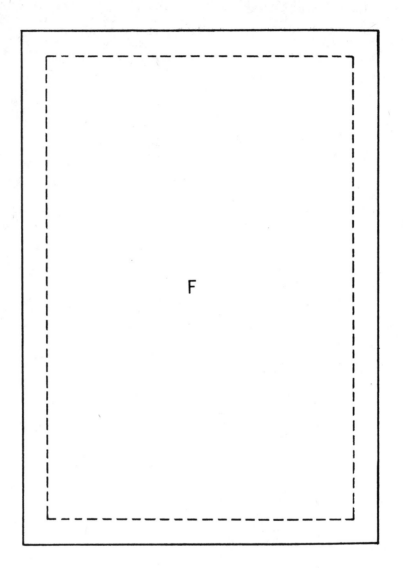

F

Virginia Reel

This design is as popular as the famous dance by the same name and as easy to master. It is attractive done in print and white or two solid colors and is sure to be a "repeat" in your quiltmaking.

Blocks: 14 inches square

Quilt top: 70 by 84 inches
30 blocks

Material you will need
Print for A, B and C units: 4 yards
White for A, D and E units: 5 yards

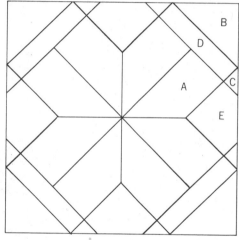

Each block requires
Print: 4 unit A
           4 unit B
           8 unit C
White: 4 unit A (cut to face opposite way from print units A)
           4 unit D
           4 unit E

Finished quilt requires
Print: 120 unit A
           120 unit B
           240 unit C
White: 120 unit A (cut to face opposite way from print units A)
           120 unit D
           120 unit E

Special cutting note
Take care that the print A units and the white A units face in the correct direction. See notation on unit A pattern.

To make one block
Join a print A unit to a white A unit at the longest side; make four such sections. Join these A-A sections to form the center of block. Then add E units to the four sides. Now join two C units and one B unit to a D unit to form a corner of the block. Make four of these sections and then sew to each side of the main section, thus forming the finished square. Press when completed.

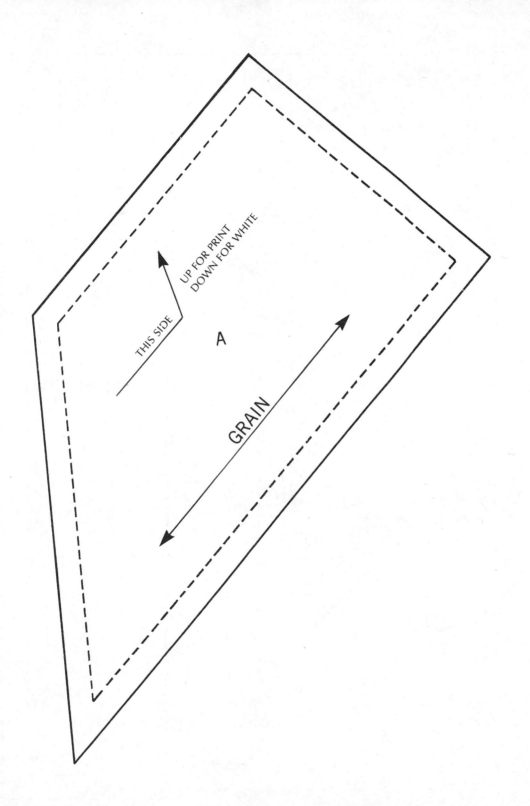

THIS SIDE

UP FOR PRINT
DOWN FOR WHITE

A

GRAIN

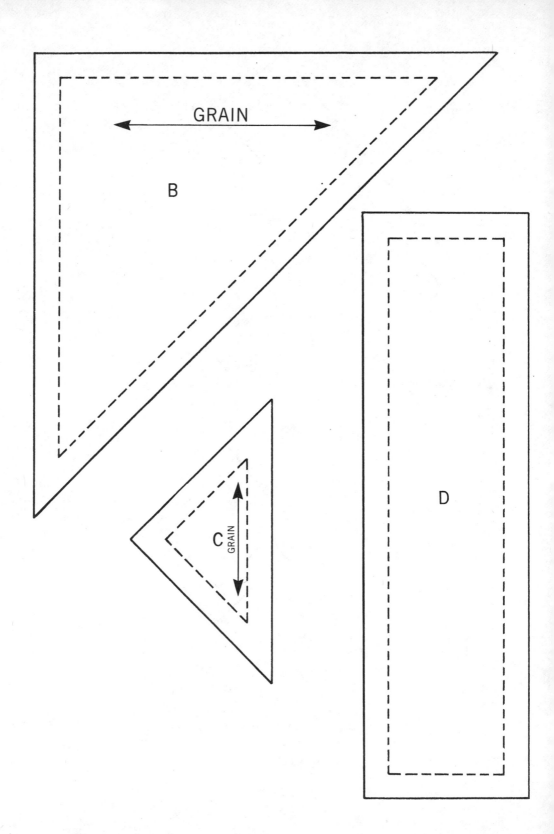

GRAIN

B

C GRAIN

D

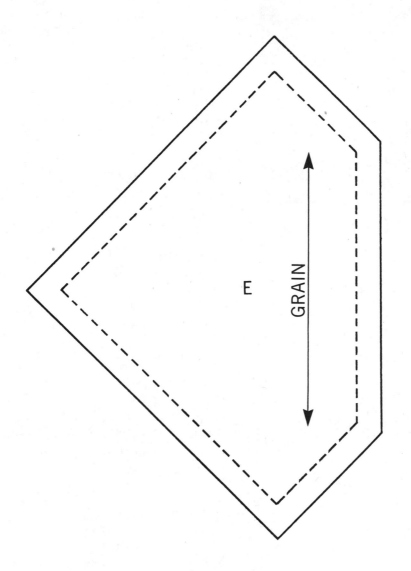

E

GRAIN

The Locked Star

Star patterns have always been popular and this new version of the star is simple to make. It is an ideal way to use checked materials and a design well worth your consideration.

Use a soft pink shade for the checked units along with light blue, white and a figured print combining all three colors.

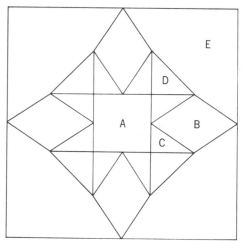

Blocks: 16 inches square

Quilt top: 80 by 96 inches
30 blocks

Material you will need
Checks for A and E units: 6 yards
Prints for B units: 2 yards
White for C units: 1½ yards
Blue for D units: 1 yard

Each block requires
Checks: 1 unit A
         4 unit E
Print: 4 unit B
White: 8 unit C (cut 4 facing left and 4 facing right)
Blue: 4 unit D

Finished quilt requires
Checks: 30 unit A
          120 unit E
Print: 120 unit B
White: 240 unit C (120 facing left and 120 facing right)
Blue: 120 unit D

Special cutting note

To cut half of the C units facing left and half facing right, either make two patterns and mark one left and the other right, or, after cutting half the pieces, turn the pattern upside down to cut the remaining half.

Use the half E unit pattern to make a full size pattern before cutting the fabric. A more accurate piece can be cut singularly rather than cutting the fabric folded.

To make one block

Join one left and one right C unit to opposite sides of a B unit; make four such C-B-C sections. Attach D units to opposite sides of two of these sections. Join the other two sections to opposite sides of the A unit. Then sew the two D-B-D sections to the B-A-B section, forming a star-shaped section. Now add E units to form a square. Press when completed.

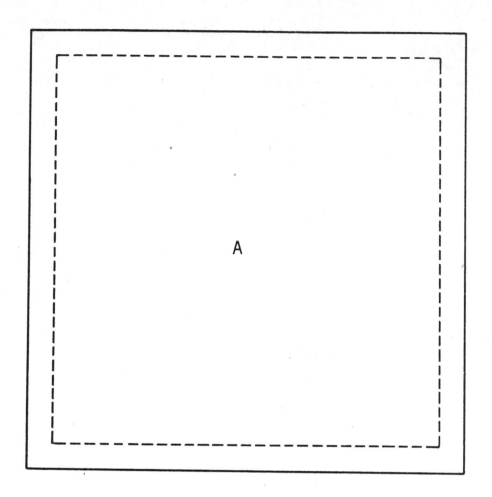

A

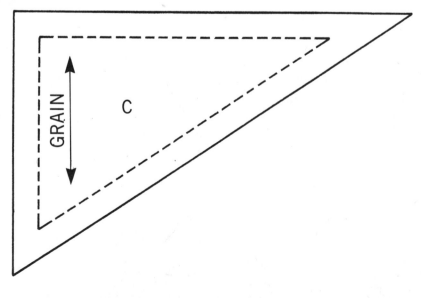

GRAIN

C

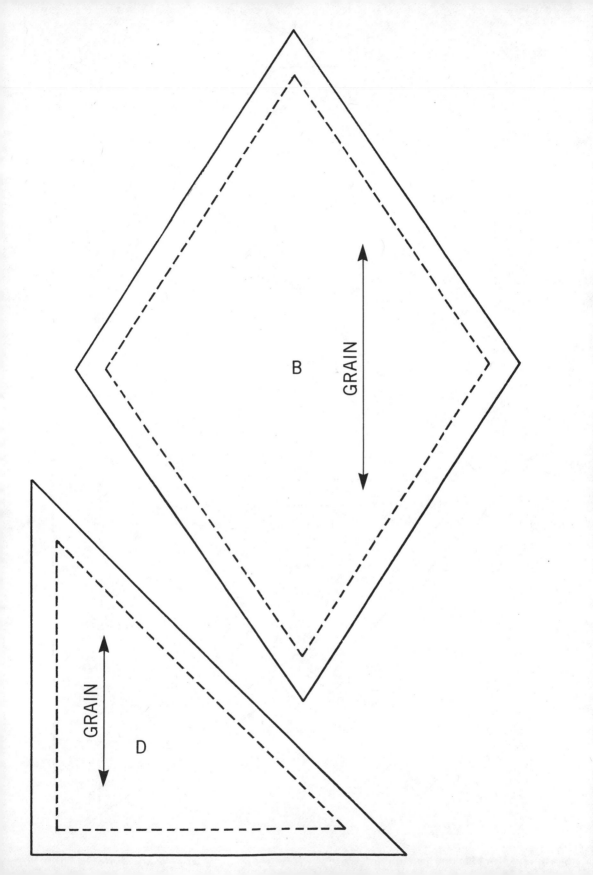

B

GRAIN

GRAIN

D

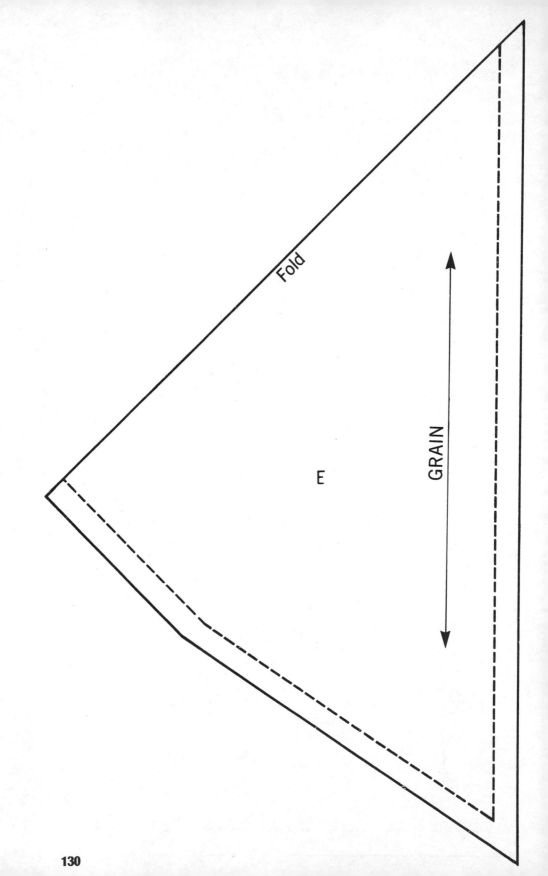

Fold

E

GRAIN

Floral Bouquet

No pattern could be more attractive than this dainty, simple appliquéd design. It demands little time to make and is sure to bring joy to its owner.

The appliquéd units look well when green is used for the small triangle, with pink or another solid color next in line and a figured print of pink and green for the third color. These colors applied to a white background make an outstanding block.

Blocks: 14 inches square

Quilt top: 70 by 98 inches
35 blocks

Material you will need
Green for A units: ¼ yard
Pink for B and D units: 4¼ yards
Print for C units: for one block, piece 6 by 9½ inches; for entire quilt, 1½ yards
White for background squares: 3¾ yards

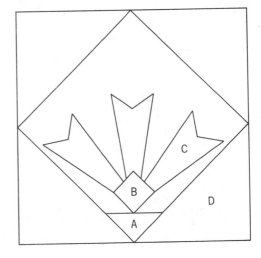

Each block requires
Green: 1 unit A
Pink: 1 unit B
       4 unit D
Print: 3 unit C
White: 1 10½-inch square

Finished quilt requires
Green: 35 unit A
Pink: 35 unit B
        140 unit D
Print: 105 unit C
White: 35 10½-inch squares

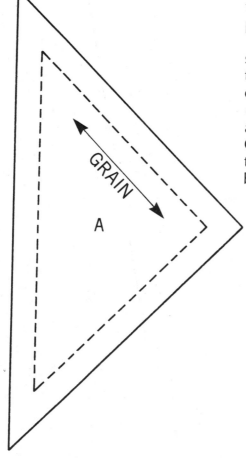

A

GRAIN

Use the half D unit pattern to make
a full size pattern before cutting
the fabric. A more accurate piece
can be cut singularly rather than
cutting the fabric folded.

To make one block
Place the A unit at the bottom
corner of the white background
square and position the B unit
diagonally above it. Following
the illustration, place the C units
at the left, top and right of the B
unit. Baste the units into place,
backstitch and press when completed. Attach the D units to the
four sides of the square and
press again.

   The seam allowances on short
sides of A unit should not be
turned under. They will be
caught in the seam when the D
units are added. The seam allowance on the shortest side of the
C units likewise should not be
turned under. They are covered
by the B unit.

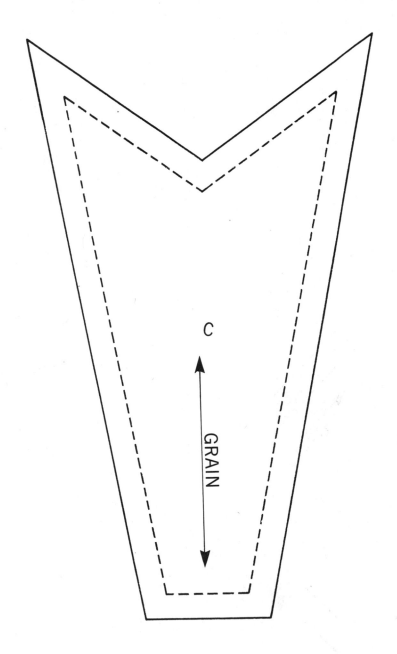

C

GRAIN

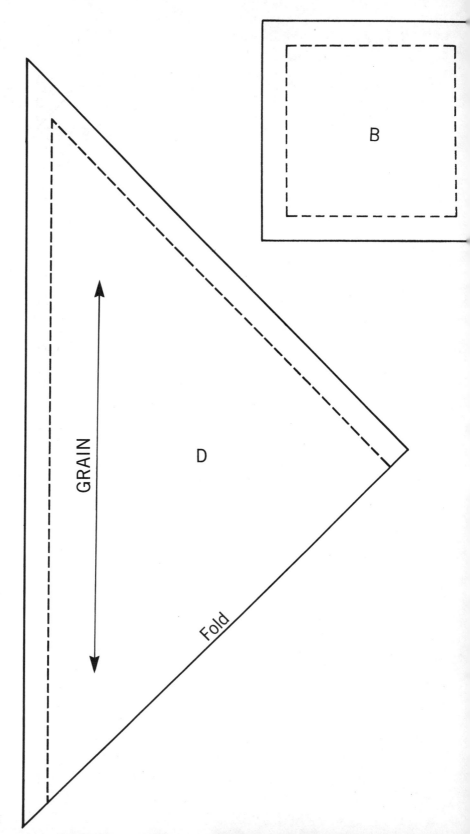

GRAIN

D

B

Fold

Eight-Pointed Star

Another star design, this one playing small stars against large stars on a solid-color background. Use your most colorful scraps throughout. No matter how varied they are, the shape of the stars and the background will make the quilt top look unified.

Quilt top: 78 by 97 inches including border
20 large stars and 12 small stars

Material you will need
Prints for large stars (A unit): piece 8½ by 3½ inches for each unit
Prints for small stars (B unit): piece 5½ by 2¼ inches for each unit
Yellow or other solid for background and border: 6 yards
Prints for border triangles: piece 6 by 4½ inches for each unit

Each star requires
8 unit A or
8 unit B

Finished quilt requires
160 unit A
 96 unit B
 68 print border triangles
 72 yellow border triangles

To assemble one star
Join the diamonds first in pairs, four such sections. Now join two pairs together making two half stars. Sew the halves together to make a whole star. This orderly piecing results in well-matched

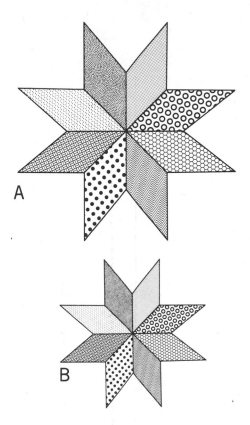

A

B

See pages 109 and 110 for color photographs of this quilt.

centers with as little bulk as possible.

To assemble the quilt top

Piece together the twenty large stars and twelve small stars. Each large star is made by joining eight A units; each small star, by joining eight B units. Press, turning under the seam allowances on the outside edges. The background is made by cutting two lengths of yellow, each measuring 90½ by 36 inches, and sewing them together to make one piece 90½ by 71½ inches. The large stars are placed on the background in four rows of five stars each, leaving about a 2¼-inch margin at the edges. There should be 18 inches from the center of one star to the center of the next. The small stars are then placed in the spaces between the large stars in four rows of three stars each. Again there should be 18 inches from the center of one small star to the center of the next. Baste all stars in place and then stitch.

To make the border, piece print and yellow triangles together in alternating fashion. For the top and bottom, use 15 print and 16 yellow triangles each, and for each side piece together 19 print and 20 yellow triangles. Attach the border to the quilt top with the print triangles inside, and then join the yellow corner triangles together to finish the quilt top. Press when completed.

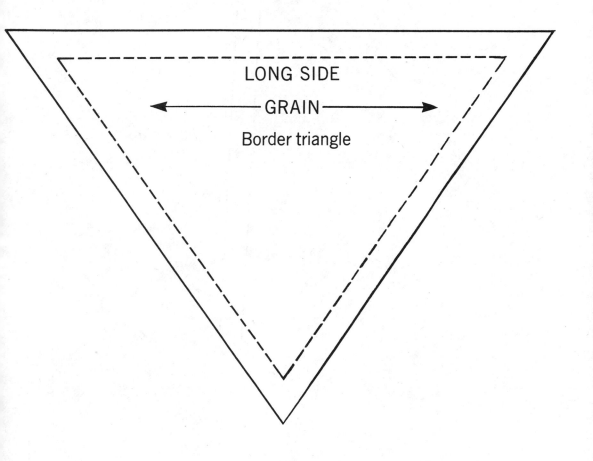

LONG SIDE

GRAIN

Border triangle

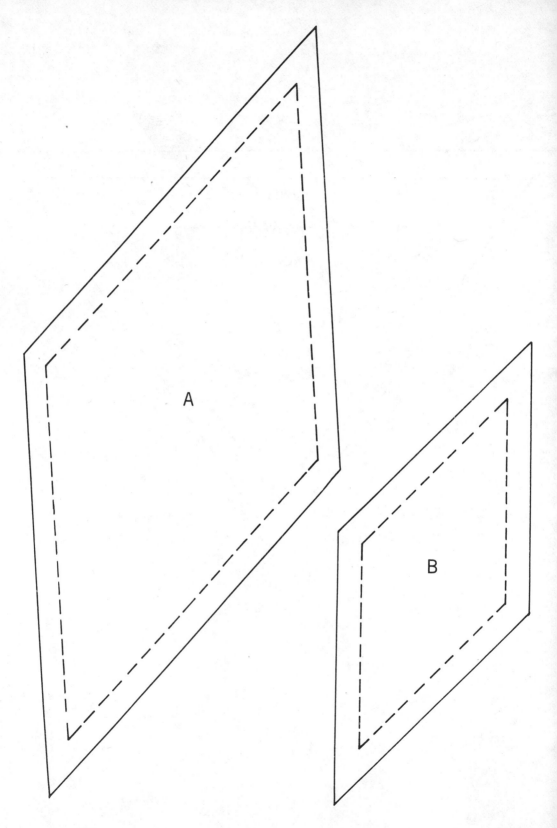

A

B

The Shooting Star

The inspiration for this pattern came quick as a flash, as a star shoots earthward from a clear sky. Just as this is a sight one marvels at and never grows tired of seeing, so with this pattern. It will grow more wonderful with every block.

Blocks: 18 inches square

Quilt top: 72 by 90 inches
20 blocks

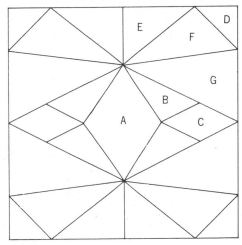

Material you will need
Yellow for A units: 1 yard
Purple for B units: 1 yard
Orange for C and F units: 3 yards
Blue for D and E units: 2 yards
Green for G units: 3 yards

Each block requires
Yellow: 1 unit A
Purple: 4 unit B (2 facing left and
         2 facing right)
Orange: 2 unit C
         4 unit F (2 facing left and
         2 facing right)
Blue: 4 unit D
         4 unit E (2 facing left and
         2 facing right)
Green: 4 unit G (2 facing left and
         2 facing right)

Finished quilt requires
Yellow: 20 unit A
Purple: 80 unit B (40 facing left
         and 40 facing right)
Orange: 40 unit C
         80 unit F (40 facing left
         and 40 facing right)

Blue: 80 unit D
       80 unit E (40 facing left
       and 40 facing right)
Green: 80 unit G (40 facing left
       and 40 facing right)

Special cutting note

To cut half the B, E, F and G units
facing left and half facing right,
either make two patterns for
each unit and mark one left and
the other right, or, after cutting
half the pieces, turn the patterns
upside down to cut the remaining half. Use the half A unit pattern and the split G unit pattern
to make full size patterns before
cutting the fabric.

To make one block

Join a left and a right B unit to adjacent sides of a C unit; then attach two facing G units. Sew the
A unit to this section, joining it
to the B units. Make a second
section like the first and attach it
to the opposite side of the A
unit. Now join a D and E unit to
an F unit following diagram;
make four of these sections. Sew
two of these sections together at
the short E unit sides to form an
oblong. Join this oblong to the
top of the main section. Join the
other two D-E-F sections and add
to the base of the main section
to form the finished block. Press
when completed.

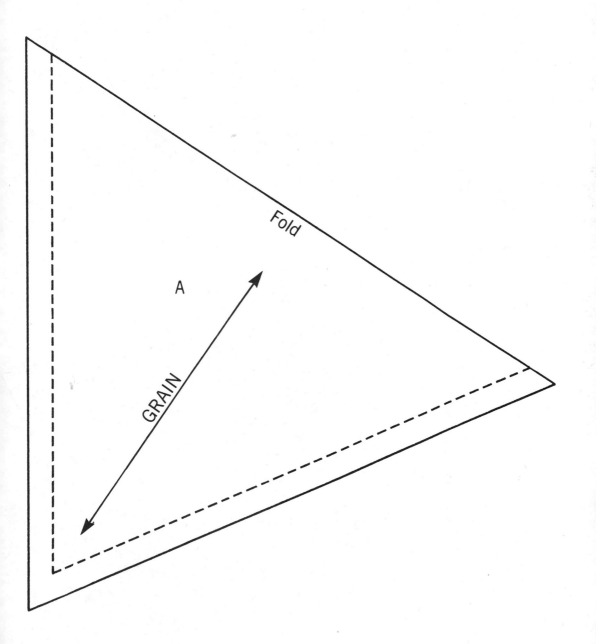

Fold

A

GRAIN

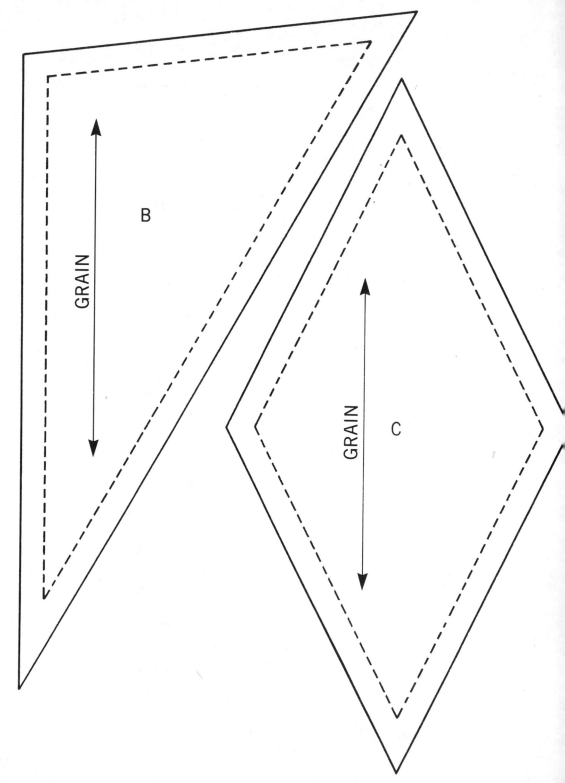

B

GRAIN

C

GRAIN

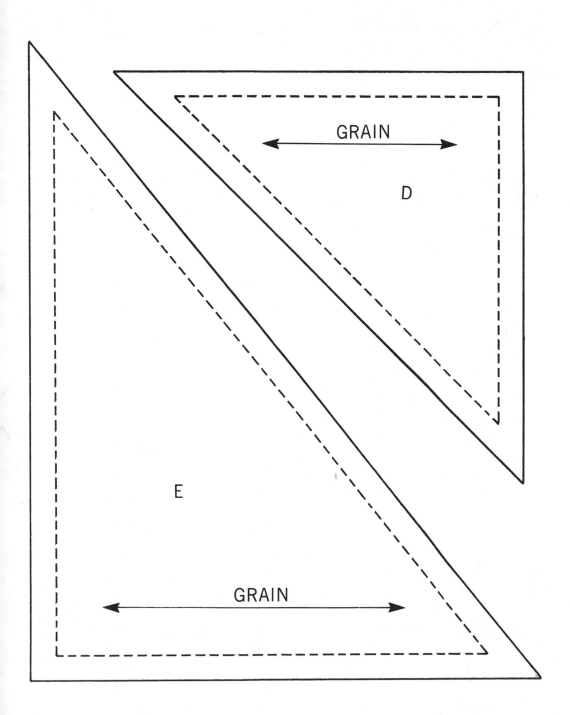

GRAIN

D

GRAIN

E

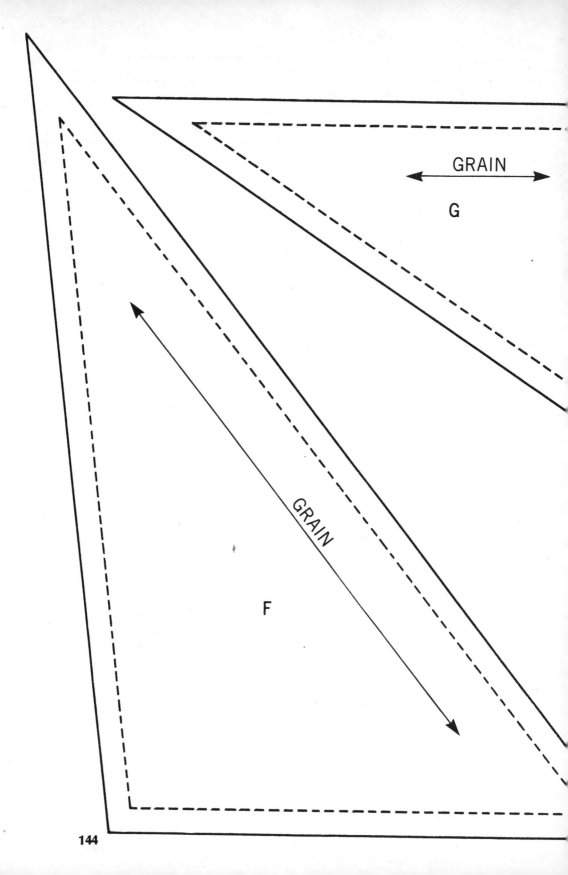

GRAIN

G

GRAIN

F

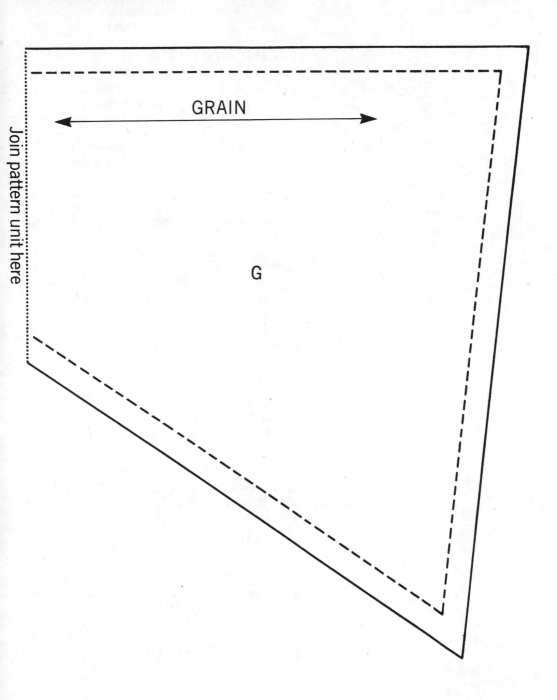

GRAIN

Join pattern unit here

G

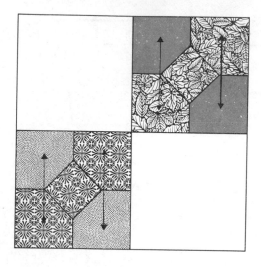

The Necktie

This old design is in great demand for its easy-to-do qualities. It has always been a great favorite and even a beginner can make it to perfection. It's an adorable design but demands separation by alternating with plain blocks or using a sashing between each block. This is a fascinating way to use odds and ends of scraps with an overall color scheme carried out in the plain unpieced blocks.

Necktie square: 4 inches square

Full block: 8 inches square

Quilt top: 80 by 91 inches without border, 86 by 97 with border
98 full blocks; 196 necktie squares and 196 plain squares

Material you will need
Print for A and B units: for each block, two pieces 3 by 8 inches
Plain color for A units: for each block, two pieces 3 by 5½ inches
Yellow or other solid for C units: for entire quilt, 3¼ yards
Dark solid color for border: large and small triangles and 3½-inch-wide strips, 2¼ yards (pieced strips) or 2⅞ yards (one-piece strips)

Necktie square requires
Plain: 2 unit A
Print: 2 unit A
       1 unit B

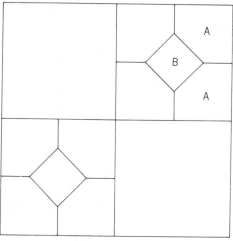

See pages 109 and 110 for color photographs of this quilt.

Each full block requires

Plain: 4 unit A
Print: 4 unit A
         2 unit B
Yellow: 2 unit C

Finished quilt requires

Plain: 392 unit A
Print: 392 unit A
             196 unit B
Yellow: 196 unit C
Dark solid: 26 large triangles, 4 small triangles and 3½-inch-wide border strips

---

Cutting the border triangles and strips

Cut the border strips first, lengthwise of the fabric, to minimize piecing these border pieces. Each strip is 3½ inches wide. Two strips should be 86½ inches long, plus a couple of extra inches for possible error adjustment, and two strips should be 97½ inches long, plus a couple of inches.

If there has been no variation in size while joining the blocks and top, the large triangles will measure 9 by 9 by 12½ inches, and the small triangles will measure 6½ by 6½ by 9¼ inches. Make patterns using these measurements and check with your top before cutting out all the pieces. Make adjustments on the patterns as needed.

To make one necktie square

Join the two print A units to opposite sides of the B unit. Then add the two plain A units to form a square. Press when completed.

To make one full block

Join a C unit to a necktie square; make two of these rectangular sections. Join the rectangular sections to form a square, following the diagram. Press.

To assemble the quilt top

Join the blocks together following the photograph on page 110. After the blocks are all sewn together, sew the large triangles to the edges with the four small triangles at the corners. Now sew on the border strips and miter the corners.

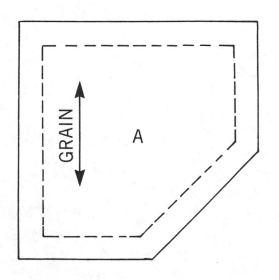

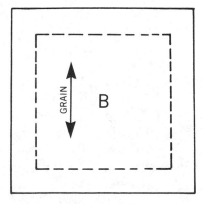

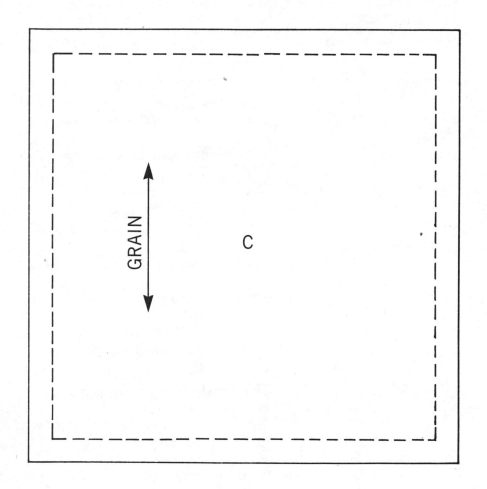

GRAIN

C

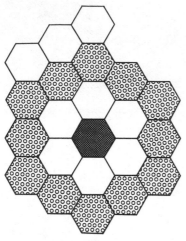

See page 198 for color photograph of this quilt.

Merry-Go-Round

Any combination of prints provides vivid interest in this lively quilt. Concentric circles of small hexagons make an abstract merry-go-round that's sure to please adults as well as children.

Quilt top: 75 by 97 inches without border; 78 by 100 inches with border
1205 units; 1 center unit, 594 white units and 610 print units

---

Material you will need
White for alternating circles: 7 yards
Solid for center unit and border: 1 yard
Prints for alternating circles: thirteen prints of various colors (see below). Each unit requires a piece 3¾ inches square.

The finished quilt top requires
White: 594 units
Solid: 1 unit and 10 yards of 3-inch-wide strips for border
Print A: 12 units (¼ yard material)
Print B: 24 units (⅜ yard)
Print C: 36 units (½ yard)
Print D: 48 units (⅝ yard)
Print E: 60 units (¾ yard)
Print F: 72 units (⅞ yard)
Print G: 84 units (1 yard)
Print H: 96 units (1⅛ yards)
Print I: 66 units (⅞ yard)
Print J: 52 units (⅝ yard)
Print K: 36 units (½ yard)

Print L: 20 units (⅜ yard)
Print M: 4 units (7½-inch square)

To assemble the quilt top

Join 6 white units in a circle, Row 1, and attach to center unit. Next, following the illustration, join the 12 print A units in a circle, Row 2, and add to main unit. Continue making circles and adding them to main unit as follows: Row 3, 18 white; Row 4, 24 print B; Row 5, 30 white; Row 6, 36 print C; Row 7, 42 white; Row 8, 48 print D; Row 9, 54 white; Row 10, 60 print E; Row 11, 66 white; Row 12, 72 print F; Row 13, 78 white; Row 14, 84 print G; Row 15, 90 white; Row 16, 96 print H. You have now completed making the full circles. Two opposite sides of this main section are the sides of the quilt top. The other four sides are the top and bottom edges to which more units are to be added.

Now join 33 white units together in a V shape and attach to one end of the main unit; repeat at other end. Using print I, make two more V shapes of 33 units each and join to the white units. Look at the photograph on page 188. The top is now complete through the blue striped units (print I). Next make four strips of 15 white units each and attach them to the print I edges. Continue adding strips to each corner as follows: 13 print J units; 11 white units; 9 print K

units; 7 white units; 5 print L u-
nits; 3 white units; 1 print M unit.
The pieced part of the quilt top is
now complete. To finish the
quilt top, make a border of the
solid-color strips and join to
quilt, placing it so that the pattern units overlap the border
edge.

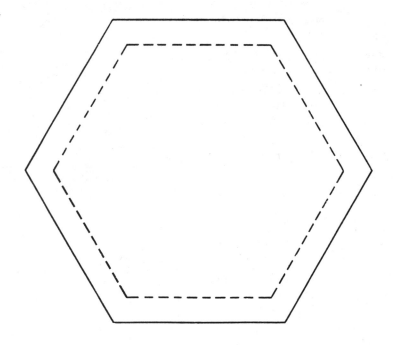

Royal Star

History tells us that this design, like several others, was brought to the Western world by the early colonists. It is handsome when done in red, white and blue with a checked center of red and white.

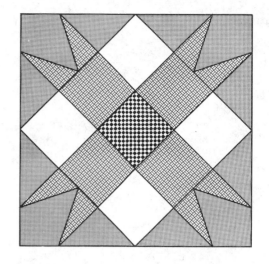

Blocks: 12 inches square

Quilt top: 72 by 84 inches
42 blocks

Material you will need
Checks for A units: ½ yard
White for A units: 1¾ yards
Figured print for A and C units: 3¼ yards
Solid color for B and D units: 3 yards

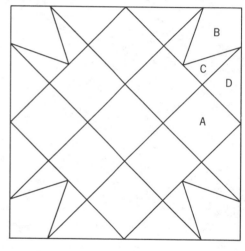

Each block requires
Checks: 1 unit A
White: 4 unit A
Print: 4 unit A
       8 unit C (4 facing left and 4 facing right)
Solid: 4 unit B
       8 unit D

Finished quilt requires
Checks: 42 unit A
White: 168 unit A
Print: 168 unit A
        336 unit C (168 facing left and 168 facing right)
Solid: 168 unit B
        336 unit D

Special cutting note

To cut half the C units facing left and half facing right, either make two patterns and mark one left and the other right, or, after cutting half the pieces, turn the pattern upside down to cut the remaining half.

To make one block

Make a square patch by joining four white, one checked and four print A units, placing the white units at the corners and the checked in the center. Press this section. Now make four triangular sections just alike, using for each one, one B unit, one left and one right C unit and two D units. Press these four sections. Then join them to the four sides of the square, thus forming the finished block. Press again when completed.

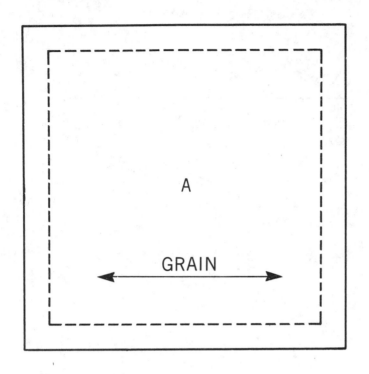

A

GRAIN

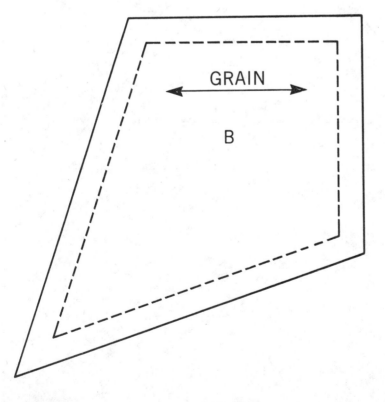

GRAIN

B

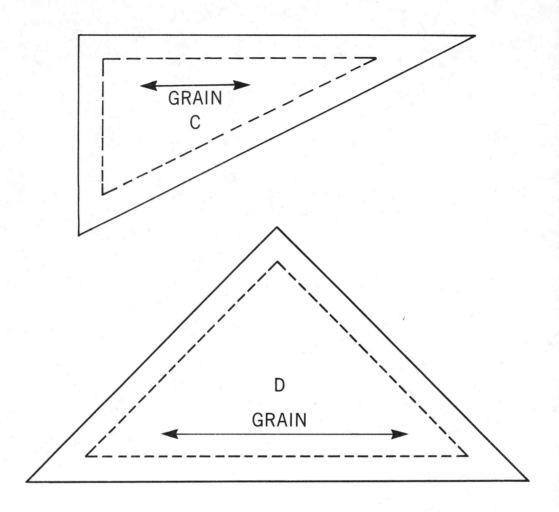

GRAIN
C

D
GRAIN

The Red Schoolhouse

Memories of days gone by or perhaps it's a quilt for your daughter. No better design could be chosen — all straight seams and a beautiful array of colors. Choose vivid colors, perhaps making each house of different colors, and separate the blocks with wide sashing. This is a quilt anyone would be proud to own.

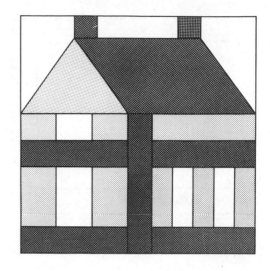

Blocks: 13 inches square

Quilt top: 77 by 95 inches (with 5-inch sashing and 5-inch border) 20 blocks
(The photograph of this quilt does not have the border.)

Material you will need
Green for A, B, D, E and G units: 1½ yards
White for A, B, E, I and K units: 1⅝ yards
Red for C, D, F, H and J units: 2 yards
White or other color for sashing: 4¼ yards

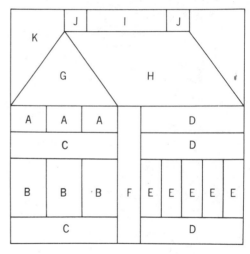

See pages 7 and 8 for color photographs of this quilt.

Each block requires
Green: 2 unit A
          2 unit B
          1 unit D
          3 unit E
          1 unit G
White: 1 unit A
          1 unit B
          2 unit E
          1 unit I
          2 unit K
Red: 2 unit C
          2 unit D

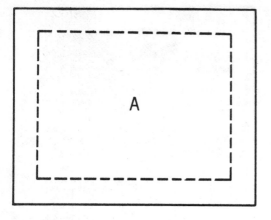

1 unit F
1 unit H
2 unit J

Finished quilt requires

Green: 40 unit A
        40 unit B
        20 unit D
        60 unit E
        20 unit G
White: 20 unit A
        20 unit B
        40 unit E
        20 unit I
        40 unit K
Red: 40 unit C
        40 unit D
        20 unit F
        20 unit H
        40 unit J

Sashing and border:

15 strips, 5½ by 13½ inches
 4 strips, 5½ by 67½ inches
 2 strips, 5½ by 77½ inches plus
 2 strips, 5½ by 95½ inches plus

Special cutting notes

Use the half G unit pattern and the split H unit pattern to make full size patterns before cutting the fabric.

If fabric chosen for K units has a right and wrong side, take care that half the units are cut to face left and half are cut to face right.

Cut sashing fabric in six 5½-inch-wide strips the full length of the fabric. Cut four 67½-inch-long strips from two of these pieces. From the remaining four pieces, cut four 13½-inch-long strips from three of them and three 13½-inch-long strips from the fourth. Leave the four long pieces that you now have left to cut for the border strips.

To make one block
Attach the green A units to opposite sides of the white A unit, short sides together. Then do the same with the B units, long sides together. Join the two C units to the top and bottom of the B unit section and add the A unit section. Now make a second section by joining the five E units, alternating colors, and then attach a red D unit to the top and bottom of this piece. Join the green D unit to the top of this piece and then add the F unit to the left side. Join this piece to first section made.

Make a third section by joining the G and H units. Add a J unit to each end of the I unit and attach to the top of the H unit. Sew the K units to the corners of this section and then join to the main section to form the finished block. Press when completed.

To assemble quilt top
Join the five rows that go across the width of the quilt, each consisting of four blocks and three 5½- by 13½-inch pieces of sashing. Join these rows to each other with the 5½- by 67½-inch sashing strips between each. After this main section of the top

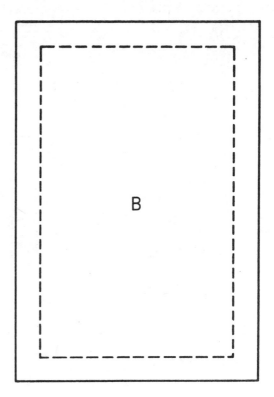

B

is sewn together, trim the four
long pieces of fabric to fit the
sides and ends. Sew them on the
main section and miter the corners.

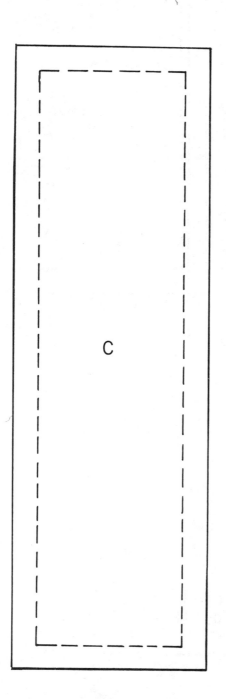

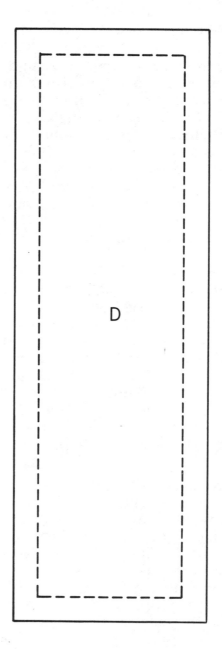

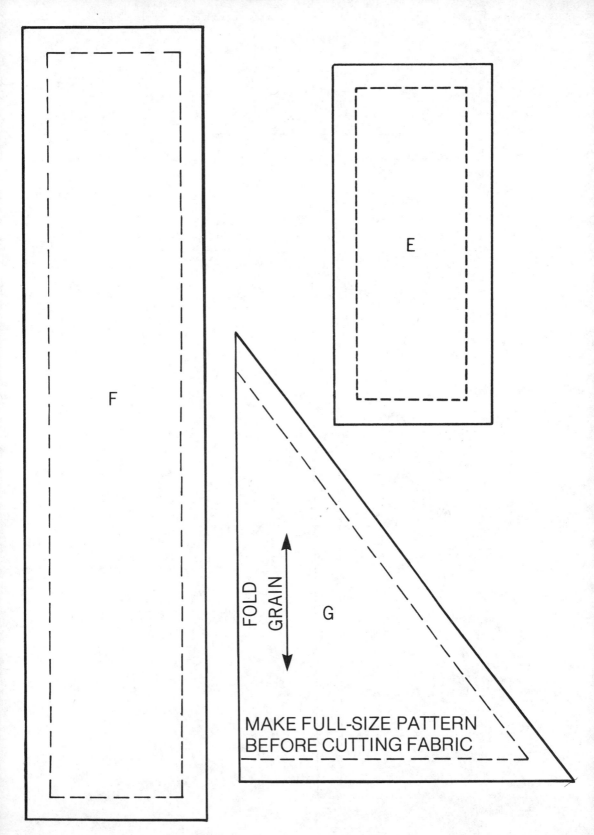

F

E

FOLD
GRAIN

G

MAKE FULL-SIZE PATTERN
BEFORE CUTTING FABRIC

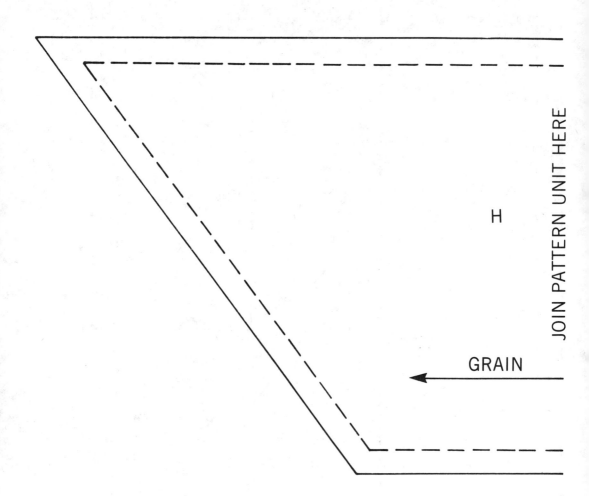

H

JOIN PATTERN UNIT HERE

GRAIN

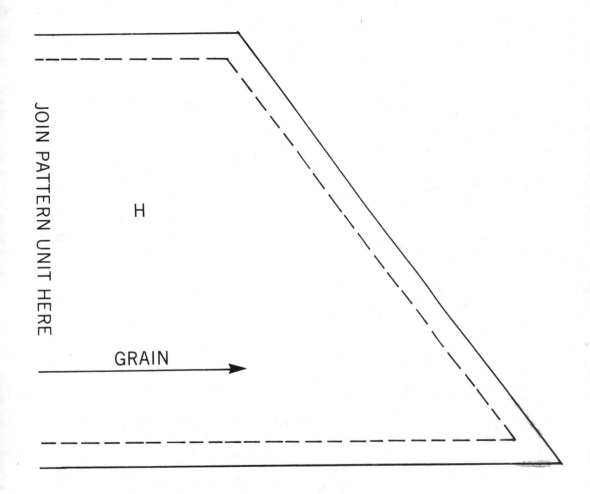

JOIN PATTERN UNIT HERE

H

GRAIN

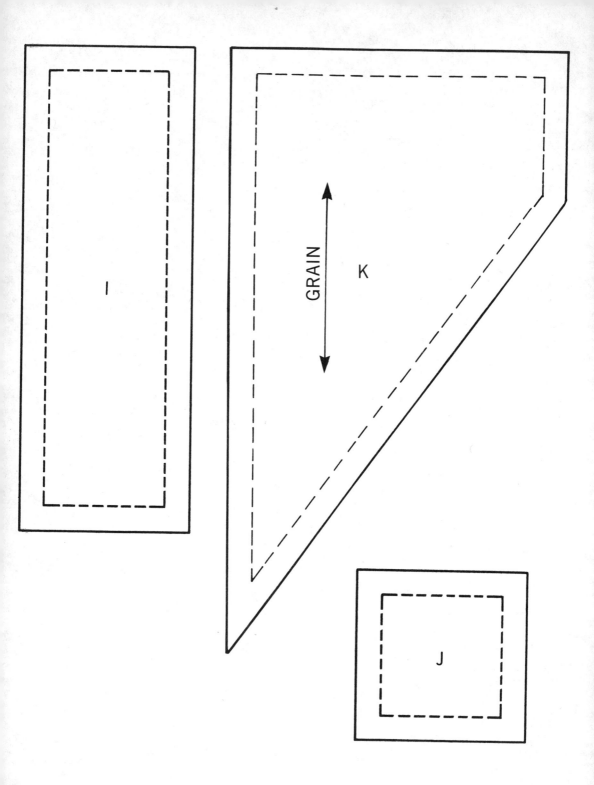

I

GRAIN

K

J

Hunter's Horns

Calling all hunters to give their opinions about this design, one of the unusual patterns that demand a figured background. Our guess is that any hunter of note will vote this a beauty. A combination of a yellow figured print for the background with two shades of blue for the horns makes a most pleasing effect. Should your favorite color be other than blue or should you desire some particular shade to match your surroundings, two shades of any color can be used with great satisfaction.

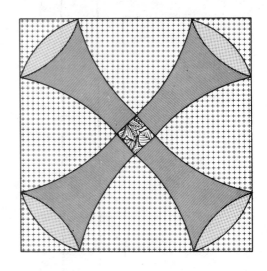

Blocks: 17½ inches square

Quilt top: 70 by 87½ inches
20 blocks

Material you will need
Print for A units: ¼ yard or 2½-inch-square piece for each block
Dark blue for B units: 4 yards
Light blue for C units: 1 yard
Figured print for background squares: 5 yards

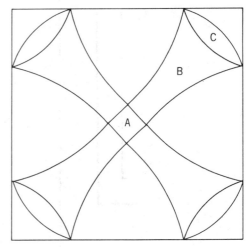

Each block requires
Print: 1 unit A
Dark blue: 4 unit B
Light blue: 4 unit C
Print: 1 18-inch square

Finished quilt requires
Print: 20 unit A
Dark blue: 80 unit B
Light blue: 80 unit C
Print: 20 18-inch squares

To make one block

Join C units to B units, making four
sections. Attach two of these
sections to opposite sides of the
A unit. Now join the other two
sections to the A unit. Press and
lay in the center of the background square. To find the center
and to give you guidelines to
properly place the A-B-C section
fold the background square in
halves, top to bottom, side to
side, and diagonally corner to
corner twice. Crease after each
fold and use these creases to lay
the horns on straight. Baste and
then appliqué to background,
and press again when completed.

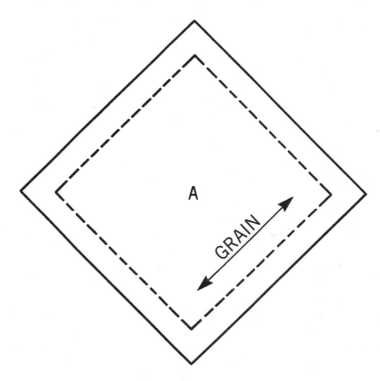

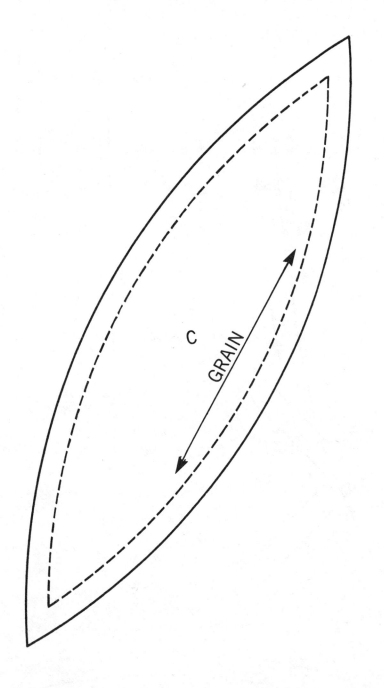

C

GRAIN

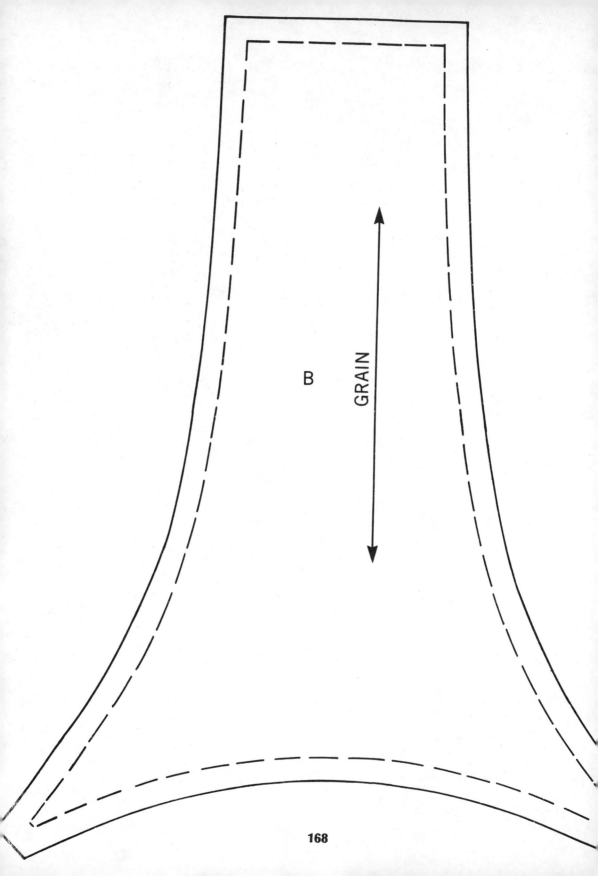

B

GRAIN

Grecian Star

With its solid-color abstract stars surrounded by patchwork circles, this handsome all-over quilt pattern is reminiscent of a kaleidoscope. It can be quilted, but is also effective when tied. Keep the stars the same light, bright color and the background dark, and use bright odd scraps for the circles.

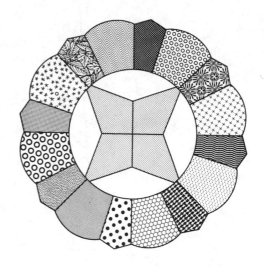

Quilt top: 78 by 93 inches with border

Stars: 25 full stars, 12 half stars and 4 quarter stars
One full star measures 12½ inches in diameter.

Material you will need
Light solid for A units (stars): 1⅛ yards
Odd scraps for B units: pieces 3½ inches square
Odd scraps for C units: pieces 3½ by 2½ inches
Total yardage for units B and C: 4½ yards
Dark solid for background and border: 6 yards

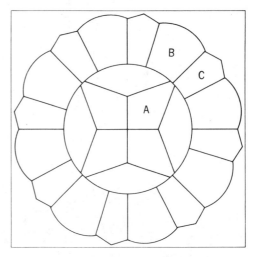

See pages 195 and 196 for color photographs of this quilt.

Each full star requires
4 unit A
8 unit B
8 unit C

Finished quilt requires
128 unit A
256 unit B
256 unit C

Border: 2 strips; 4 by 78½ inches
2 strips; 4 by 93½ inches

To make the stars
Make the twenty-five full stars as follows: piece together four A units to make a center star. Then make an outer circle by alternating eight B and eight C units. Refer to the illustration and baste the four points of the star to the circle. The twelve half stars are made in the same fashion, each consisting of two A units, four B units and four C units. The four quarter stars are each composed of one A unit, two B units and two C units.

To assemble the quilt top
Make the background by cutting two pieces 86 inches long and joining together to form one piece measuring 71½ by 86 inches. Now place the four quarter stars on the corners, matching the edges, and three half stars at the top and bottom and four at each side. Baste in place. Now position the twenty-five full stars on the background, as in the illustration on page 196, and baste. Stitch the stars in place and press. A four-inch border of the background material with mitered corners is now added to all sides of the quilt top to give a finished look.

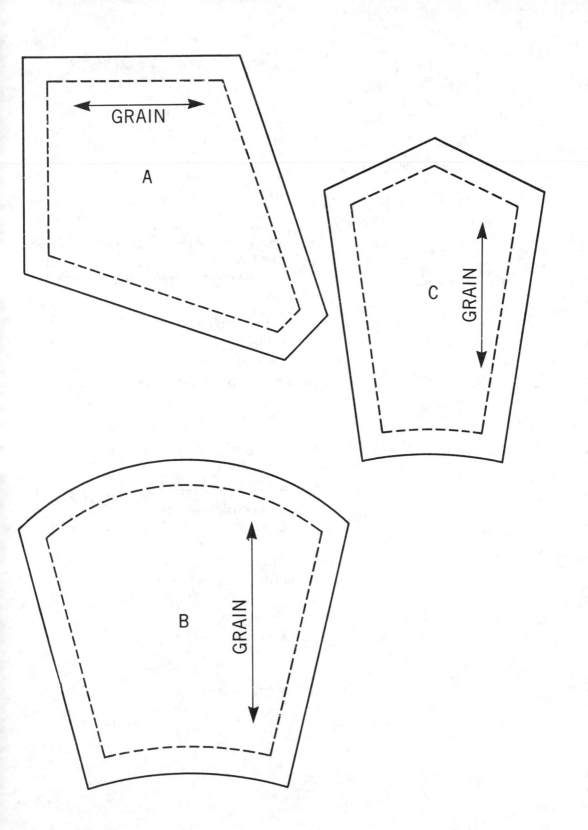

The Floral Wreath

The Floral Wreath is an example of the beauty of floral appliqué, a lovely creation and one well worth the time and work involved. One can derive a great deal of satisfaction in owning a coverlet such as this. Pink flowers, blue flowers, medium green leaves and stems make a wonderful combination. In many cases a gay figured print has been used for the larger units and a contrasting color for the smaller flower petals.

Blocks: 17½ inches square

Quilt top: 70 by 87½ inches
20 blocks

Material you will need
Green for A and B units: 1 yard
Blue for C units: 1 yard
Pink or print for D units: 1¾ yards
Plain color for background squares:
  5 yards

Each block requires
Green: 4 unit A
            4 unit B
Blue: 16 unit C
Pink: 4 unit D
Plain: 1 18-inch square

Finished quilt requires
Green: 80 unit A
            80 unit B
Blue: 320 unit C
Pink: 80 unit D
Plain: 20 18-inch squares

To make one block

Prepare background square by folding and creasing the block in eighths: top to bottom, side to side, and corner to corner twice. These creases will serve as guidelines to evenly position the pattern pieces. Place four A units at right angles at the center of the background patch. Position B units facing toward the corners, with points 1½ inches from the center. The D units are placed at the corner points of the B units, and the C units are in section formation at the ends of the A units. Baste all into position and appliqué to background. Press when completed.

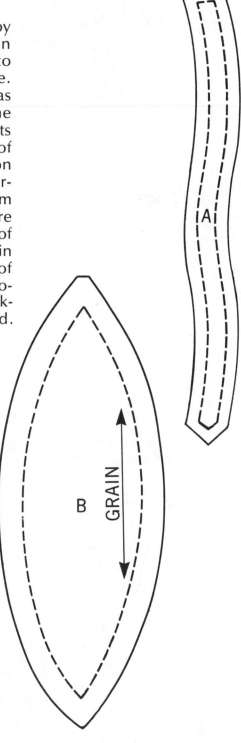

A

B GRAIN

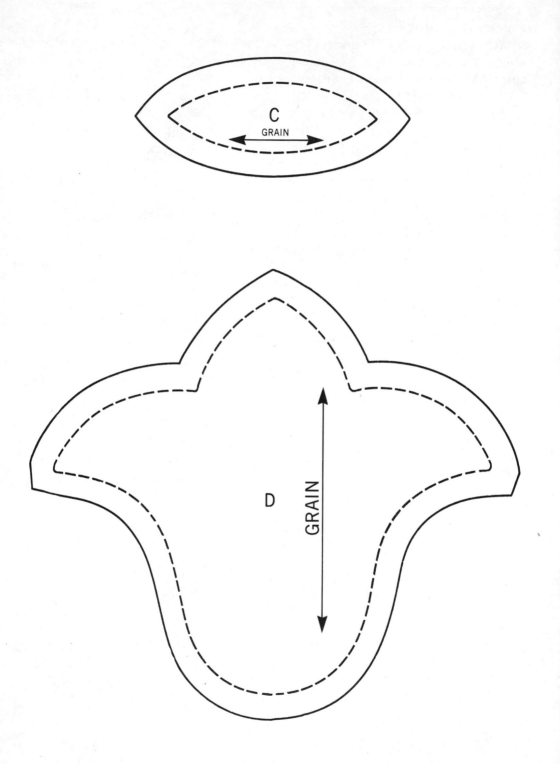

C

GRAIN

D

GRAIN

Basket Design

The ever-popular basket design is on parade again with two little bluebirds to bring you happiness. A combination of pieced work and appliqué, this is a most interesting pattern and one to be proud of. Here we do not designate all the colors, although tradition says that blue is for birds of happiness, green for the leaves and stems, a yellow shade for the flower and bud and a plain shade and a print for the basket. Each basket may be of different colors to add zest and appeal; in this case other colors could be used for the flower and bud. Just be sure they correspond with the colors in the basket units.

Blocks: 17½ inches square

Quilt top: 70 by 87½ inches
20 blocks

Material you will need
Print for A units: ⅞ yard
Plain color for A, B and C units: 1½ yards
Blue for D units: ½ yard
Green for E, F and H units: ½ yard
Yellow for G and I units: ½ yard
White for J unit: piece 10 inches square
Plain color for background squares: 5 yards
Dark blue embroidery floss — optional

Each block requires
Print: 8 unit A
Plain: 10 unit A
           2 unit B (1 facing left and 1 facing right)
           2 unit C (1 facing left and 1 facing right)

Blue: 2 unit D (1 facing left and
          1 facing right)
Green: 2 unit E
          1 unit F
          5 unit H
Yellow: 1 unit G
          4 unit I
White: 1 unit J
Plain: 1 18-inch square

Finished quilt requires

Print: 160 unit A
Plain: 200 unit A
          40 unit B (20 facing left
          and 20 facing right)
          40 unit C (20 facing left
          and 20 facing right)
Blue: 40 unit D (20 facing left
          and 20 facing right)
Green: 40 unit E
          20 unit F
          100 unit H
Yellow: 20 unit G
          80 unit I
White: 20 unit J
Plain: 20 18-inch squares

To make one block

Join the plain-color and print A
  units together to form the basket. Note that the top of the basket is four plain-color units while
  the base is of two print units.
  Press and then place this section
  in the center of the background
  square, two inches from the bottom edge. Then join together
  the B and C units to form the
  handle, press and place on top
  of the basket. Place the D units
  on either side of the handle.

Now place the E units at the top of the basket between the B units, with the F and G units at the top of the right E unit and the I and J units at the top of the left. Place two H units above the I units as shown and the remaining three H units at the base of the E units. Baste all units into place and hem to the background. Embroidery floss, 4 strands, may be used to put a satin stitch eye and an outline stitch wing on the birds. Press when completed.

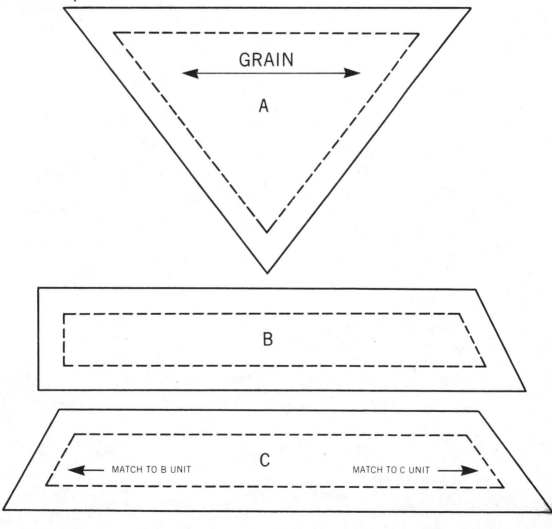

GRAIN

A

B

C

MATCH TO B UNIT

MATCH TO C UNIT

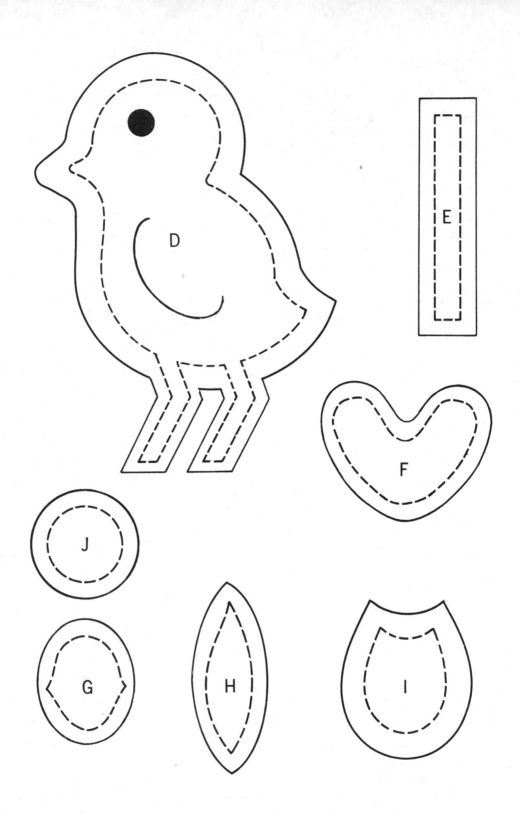

D

E

F

J

G

H

I

Mohawk Trail

An arresting and unique pattern, this is also one of the oldest. It is particularly striking when white is used as the background color and two-inch squares of white are inserted at the intersections of the sashing. The sashing itself, when done in a dark solid color, is effective as a border.

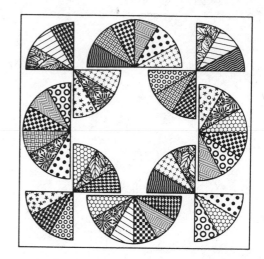

Blocks: 17 inches square

Quilt top: 68 by 85 inches without sashing; 78 by 97 inches with sashing
20 blocks

Material you will need
White for background squares and sashing: 5⅛ yards
Assorted prints for pattern units: pieces 2¾ by 4¾ inches
Total yardage for pattern units: 5½ yards
Dark solid for sashing: 2 yards
Black embroidery floss

Each block requires
48 pattern units
1 17½-inch background square

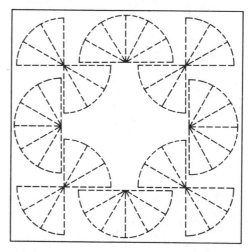

See pages 113 and 114 for color photographs of this quilt. An all over variation of this pattern is pictured on pages 111 and 114.

Finished quilt requires
960 pattern units
20 17½-inch background squares
49 solid sashing units; 2½ by 17½ inches
30 white sashing squares; 2½ by 2½ inches

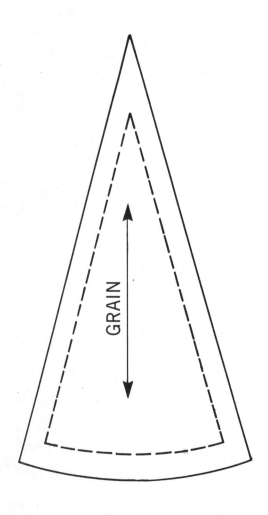

GRAIN

To make one block
Piece together eight sections of three pattern units and four sections of six pattern units. Place these units on the background square, following the diagram, leaving ¾-inch margin at the edges. Baste units in place and then stitch. Now outline each unit with a running stitch using 4 strands of black embroidery floss.

To assemble the quilt top
Cut forty-nine solid-color sashing units, each measuring 2½ by 17½ inches, and thirty 2½-inch white squares. Then join the quilt blocks together with solid-color units to form four strips of five blocks each, attaching sashing units to the top and bottom of each strip as well. Next make five long sashing pieces, each alternating six white squares and five solid units. Join the quilt top together by attaching these long sashing strips to the block units. Press when completed.

Periwinkles

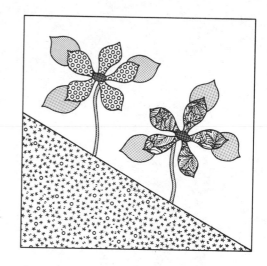

Gay, dancing periwinkles prancing along across a coverlet. What could be more charming? All the shades of pink, red and orchid can find a definite place here. The portion of the background that demands a print adds variety to the quilt's appearance.

Collect all the colors available and the gayest coverlet imaginable will be the result. You can use different colors for the flower petals and background prints in each block. Or, if you wish to emphasize a specific color, choose one figured print for all the backgrounds with colors that are in keeping with the green leaves and flower centers. In this way you can carry a definite color idea throughout every block.

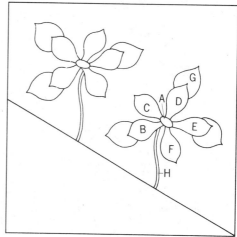

Blocks: 16 inches square

Quilt top: 80 by 96 inches
30 blocks

Material you will need
Brown for A units (centers): ⅛ yard
Print or solid for B-F units (flower petals): piece 7 by 11 inches for each flower
Green for G and H units (leaves and stems): 1½ yards
White for background: 5½ yards
Print for background: triangular piece 16½ by 10½ by 19½ inches for each block, or 2½ yards for entire quilt

Each block requires
Brown: 2 unit A
Prints: 2 sets unit B-F
Green: 6 unit G
        2 unit H

White: 1 background piece 6½ by
        16½ by 16½ by 19½
Print: 1 background triangle 16½
        by 10½ by 19½

Finished quilt requires

Brown: 60 unit A
Prints: 60 sets unit B-F
Green: 180 unit G
        60 unit H
White: 30 background pieces
Prints: 30 background triangles

To make one block

Place H units at even intervals
across long edge of white
background piece. Arrange one
set of flower petal units (B-F) at
top of each H unit, using one
print or solid color for each
flower. Then position an A unit
at center of each flower. Place
one G unit at the outer edge of
three petal units in each flower.
Baste all units into place and
then stitch to background. Overlap the triangular print unit onto
the white portion and stitch in
place. Press when completed.

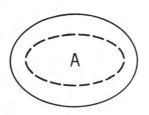

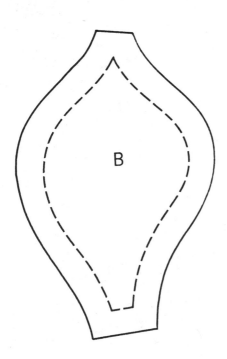

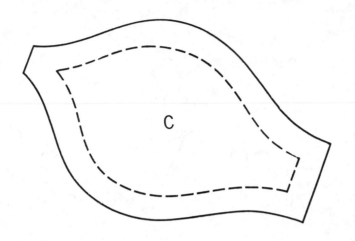

C

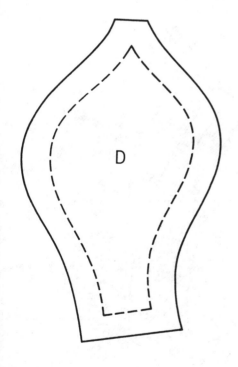

D

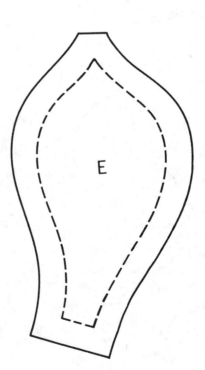

E

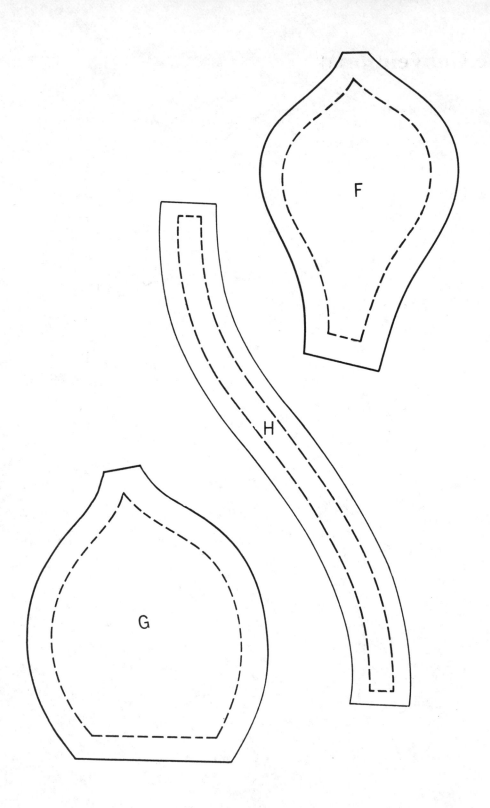

The Conventional

This design is unique in appearance, lovely in its arrangement of colors and simple to make. All this adds up to a delightful pattern. A newcomer to the quilt world, it already has been voted a "special" by experts. White is usually used for the background, although your favorite plain color could be used. Yellow with a multicolored print are the other two colors that make a charming effect for this motif. Be sure to cut half of the C units pointing up and half pointing down so the design of the print will not be reversed.

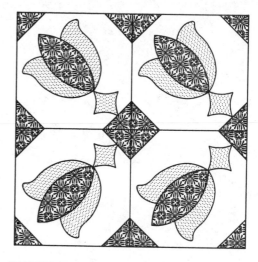

Blocks: 8½ inches square

Quilt top: 76½ by 93½ inches
99 blocks

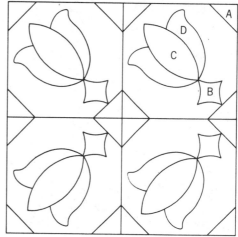

Material you will need
Print for A and C units: 3 yards
Yellow for B and D units: 3 yards
White for background squares: 6¼
yards

Each block requires
Print: 4 unit A
           1 unit C
Yellow: 1 unit B
           2 unit D (1 facing left and 1
           facing right)
White: 1 9-inch square

Finished quilt requires
Print: 396 unit A
           99 unit C
Yellow: 99 unit B
           198 unit D (99 facing left
           and 99 facing right)
White: 99 9-inch squares

To make one block

Prepare background square by folding on the diagonal, corner to corner, and crease. This crease will be used as a guideline for positioning the C and B units. Appliqué an A unit to each corner of the background square. It is only necessary to turn under and sew the long side. The two short sides need only be basted because they should line up with the cut edges of the background and will be sewn when the blocks are joined. Place the B unit at one of the corner A units, with the points touching the halfway mark of the A unit and the crease. The C unit is placed at the opposite point of the B unit, along the crease. The D units are placed to the left and right sides of the C unit. Baste all units into place and appliqué into position. Press when completed.

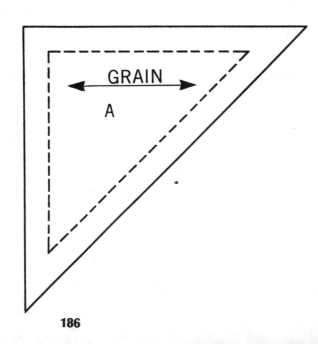

GRAIN

A

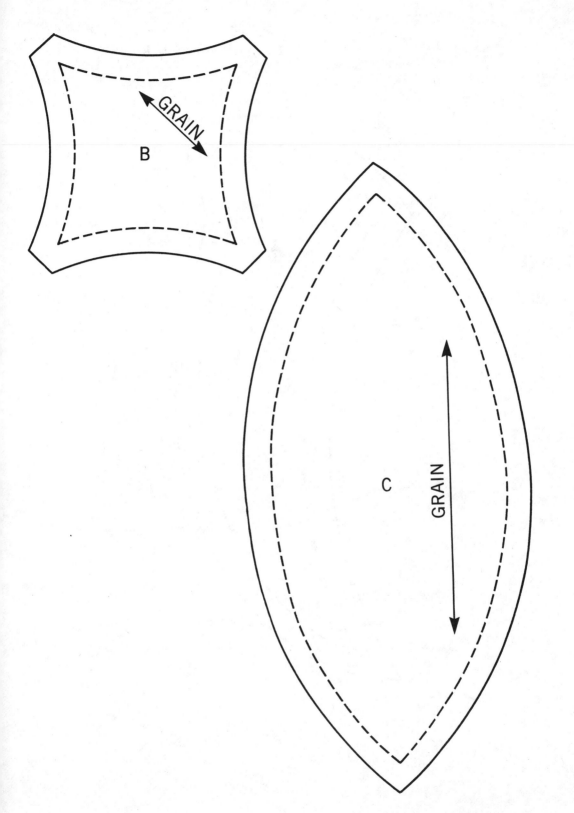

B

GRAIN

C

GRAIN

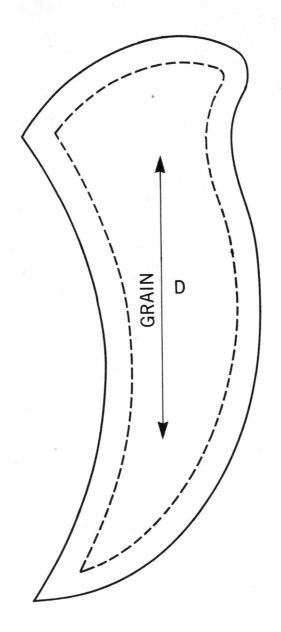

GRAIN

D

The Swinging Star

Stars and more stars — they never grow out of date and are always appreciated. This new-era design is a lovely creation and one that will gain in popularity as time goes on. Why not use your own favorite colors and have your star quilt swing along with your color scheme? The original design was made with brown and pink units for the oval sections and a blue center, with a blue ribbon effect to match the center. This makes a most charming arrangement.

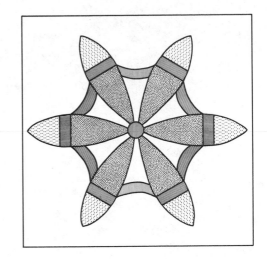

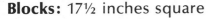

Blocks: 17½ inches square

Quilt top: 70 by 87½ inches
20 blocks

Material you will need
Blue for A, C and E units: 1¼ yards
Brown for B units: 1½ yards
Pink for D units: ⅞ yard
Plain color for background squares:
  5 yards

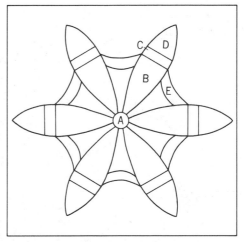

Each block requires
Blue: 1 unit A
           6 unit C
           6 unit E
Brown: 6 unit B
Pink: 6 unit D
Plain: 1 18-inch square

Finished quilt requires
Blue: 20 unit A
          120 unit C
          120 unit E
Brown: 120 unit B
Pink: 120 unit D
Plain: 20 18-inch squares

To make one block

Make six oval sections by joining one B unit, one C unit and one D unit, in the order given. Place the A unit in the center of the background square and then place the six oval sections around it. The E units are placed between the oval sections, reaching from one to another. Baste all the units into place and stitch to the background. Press when completed.

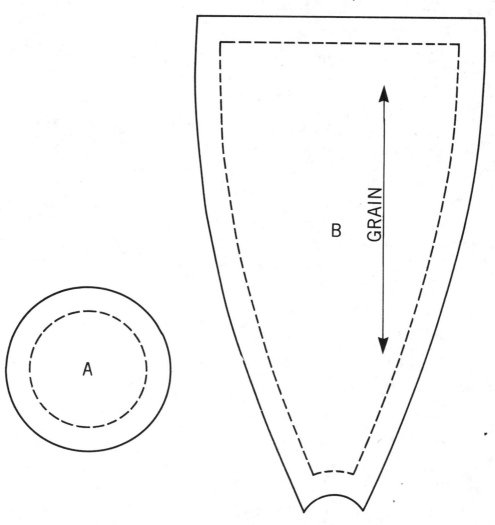

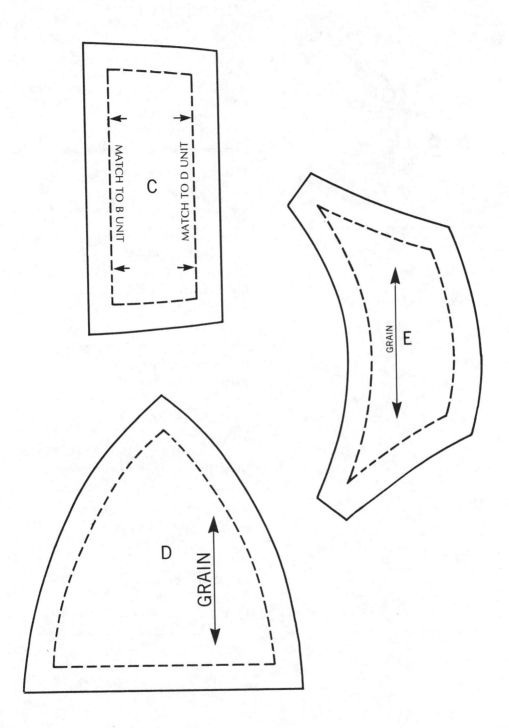

C

MATCH TO B UNIT

MATCH TO D UNIT

E

GRAIN

D

GRAIN

Poinsettia

A Christmas block that is sure to please the year round. The red and green combination is always appealing. The large units add to its attractiveness by making it a quick project for those who have limited time for such work.

Blocks: 17½ inches square

Quilt top: 70 by 87½ inches
20 blocks

Material you will need
Red for A, B and D units: 3½ yards
Green for C and E units: 1½ yards
White for background squares: 5
   yards

Each block requires
Red: 1 unit A
          16 unit B
          4 unit D
Green: 4 unit C
          8 unit E
White: 1 18-inch square

Finished quilt requires
Red: 20 unit A
        320 unit B
        80 unit D
Green: 80 unit C
        160 unit E
White: 20 18-inch squares

To make one block

Place the A unit in the center of the background square, with the 16 B units spaced evenly around it. Now place one C unit in each corner, with the narrow end just under the edge of a B unit. The D units are placed at the ends of the C units and the E units on the left and right of the stems. Baste all units into place and stitch to background. Press when completed.

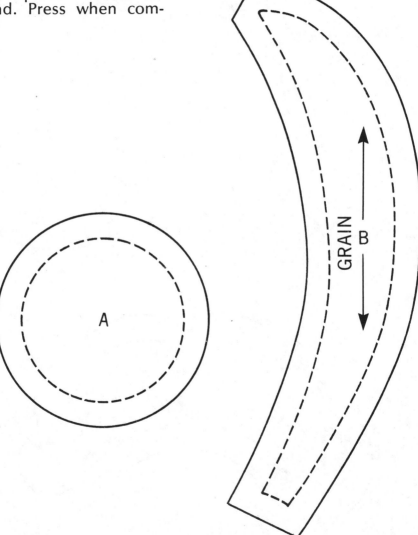

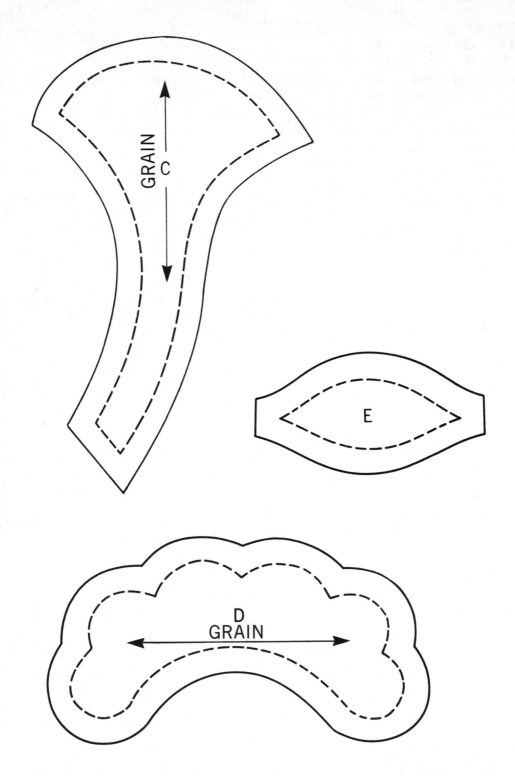

GRAIN
C

E

D
GRAIN

Grecian Star (left) and Six-Pointed Star (right)

Six-Pointed Star
(Pattern on page 89)

Grecian Star
(Pattern on page 158)

Opposite: Broken Sash

Broken Sash
(Pattern on page 49)

Merry-Go-Round
(Pattern on page 143)

The Dresden Plate

This design has been known by several different names: "The Friendship," "The Sunflower" and "The Bride's Quilt." Few designs have been more used, better liked or can give a wider range of colors and color combinations. Its easy making leaves no dull moments, as new interest develops in every stage.

Here are a few possible color arrangements that will aid in giving different aspects to your materials. One can make each center a different color, or every center throughout the entire quilt top can be the same. The petals can be of as many different colors and prints as one would wish. Any petal arangement is effective. One can make every second petal the same color as the center; every second, third or fourth petal can be the same; or every unit can be different. Just be sure to plan an overall harmonious arrangement for your quilt.

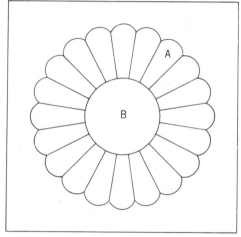

See pages 111 and 112 for color photographs of this quilt.

Quilt top: 71 by 90 inches
20 plates
Individual plates measure 13¼ inches in diameter

Material you will need

A units: piece 4½ by 3 inches for each unit.
Total yardage for A units: 4½ yards
B units: piece 6½ inches in diameter for each unit; ¾ yard for entire quilt
Solid color for background: 5 yards

Each plate requires
20 unit A
 1 unit B

Finished quilt requires

400 unit A
 20 unit B

To make one plate

Join all twenty A units to form a ring and press. Overlap the B unit in the center. Baste the two pieces into place and stitch. Press when completed.

To assemble the quilt top

Cut the background yardage in half and sew together to make one piece measuring 71 by 90 inches. Now position the twenty plates evenly on the background and appliqué in place. In your quilting, follow the design of the pattern units on the plates and fill in the background with a simple all-over quilting design.

This quilt may also be made in squares, with or without sashing, and you may also vary the overall design by combining half plates, quarter plates and full plates. The quilt on page 112 has a print back with a solid sashing border and print corners for added interest.

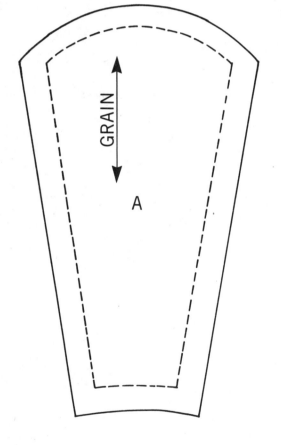

GRAIN

A

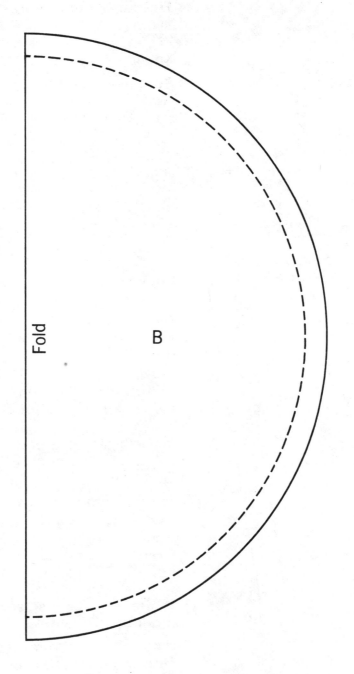

Fold

B

Blossoms and Berries

This is a design that demands more than a passing glance. It also is one that every needlewoman will want to make just for the sheer joy of its marvelous arrangement. Red berries and blue flowers with green leaves and stems will display this design's full charm and beauty. The flower centers of course should be of the same shade as the berries if this combination is used. If one prefers, brown could be used for the stems and berries. With the green leaves, any color flowers would then be tasteful for this particular pattern.

Blocks: 17½ inches square

Quilt top: 70 by 87½ inches
20 blocks

Material you will need
Blue for A units: 1¼ yards
Green for B units: ½ yard
Red for C and D units: 1¼ yards
White for background squares: 5
   yards
6 packages of green narrow bias
   binding or ribbon for the stems
Green embroidery floss

Each block requires
Blue: 16 unit A
Green: 8 unit B
Red: 24 unit C
           4 unit D
White: 1 18-inch square
Binding: 50 inches

Finished quilt requires
Blue: 320 unit A
Green: 160 unit B

Red: 480 unit C
            80 unit D
White: 20 18-inch squares
Binding: 28 yards

To make one block

First place the 50 inches of bias binding on the background block in an arrangement that suits you, being sure to leave free ends on which to place the flowers and berries. Refer to the illustrations for suggestions. Baste. Place groups of six berries at four of the free ends. The four flower units, each consisting of four A units around a D unit, are placed at random to suit you. The B units are likewise placed as you wish. After placing the units to suit your taste, baste them into place and stitch to background. Embroider the lines in the B units with a running stitch, using 3 strands of floss. Press when completed.

Each block should be appliquéd in such a manner that the stems flow smoothly from block to block for a harmonious arrangement on the quilt top.

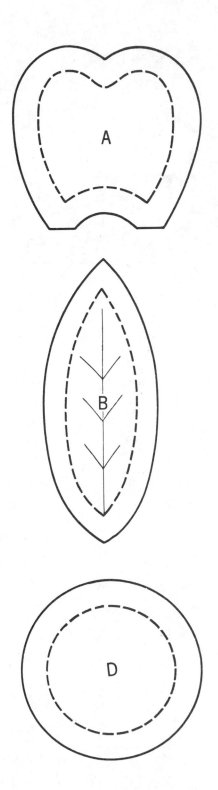

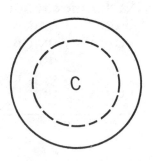

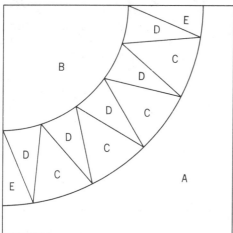

The Baby Bunting

This rare, old, complex pattern demands exactness in every detail. Don't be frightened, it's not so difficult. If you cut accurately, sew carefully and exercise patience the pattern will go together nicely. The units are sewn into squares, each one being exactly the same. The Baby Bunting pattern requires joining the block sections in the order illustrated here. Note the similarity to the Mohawk Trail pattern on page 179. This is a beautiful pattern when completed regardless of the colors used.

Blocks: 8 inches square

Completed pattern section: 16 blocks, 32 by 32 inches square

Quilt top: 80 by 96 inches
120 blocks
6 pattern sections (96 blocks) and 24 additional blocks for added width

Material you will need
Blue for A units: 4½ yards
White for B, C and E units: 6½ yards
Purple for D units: 2 yards

Each block requires
Blue: 1 unit A
White: 1 unit B
             4 unit C
             2 unit E
Purple: 5 unit D

Finished quilt top requires

Blue: 120 unit A
White: 120 unit B
           480 unit C
           240 unit E
Purple: 600 unit D

Special cutting notes

Use the half A unit pattern to make a full size pattern before cutting the fabric for a more accurate piece rather than cutting the fabric on the fold.

If the fabric chosen for the E units has a right and wrong side, half of the units must be cut facing left and half facing right.

To make one block

Join C and D units together with an E unit at each end. Sew this section to the A unit. The B unit is then joined at the base of the main section to form a square. Press when completed.

To assemble the quilt top

All 120 blocks should be made before joining them together. Join 16 blocks to form the completed pattern section, following the illustration carefully. Make six of these sections. Join these six sections, two across and three down, to form the main part of the top. This should measure 64 by 96 inches and will do nicely as is for a twin size bed. For additional width, the remaining 24 blocks can be joined 12 to each long side. The placement of these blocks should be done with care to avoid an incomplete pattern appearance. It is suggested that the order of the row of blocks that would join the edge if a full section were to be added be repeated on corresponding sides.

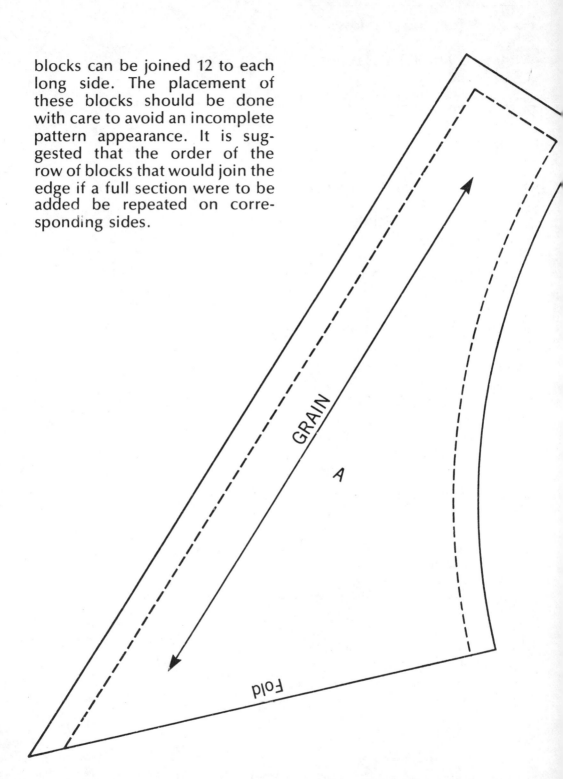

GRAIN

A

Fold

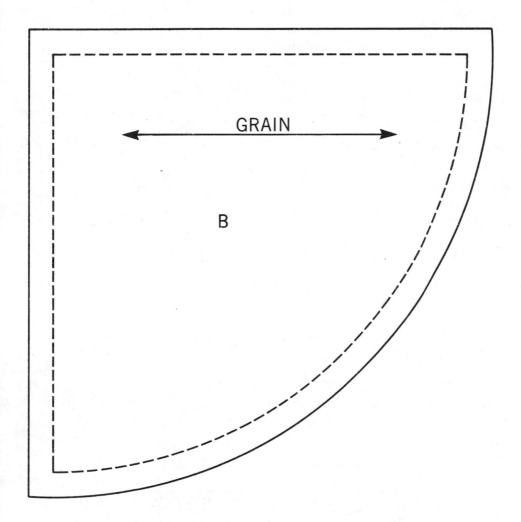
GRAIN

B

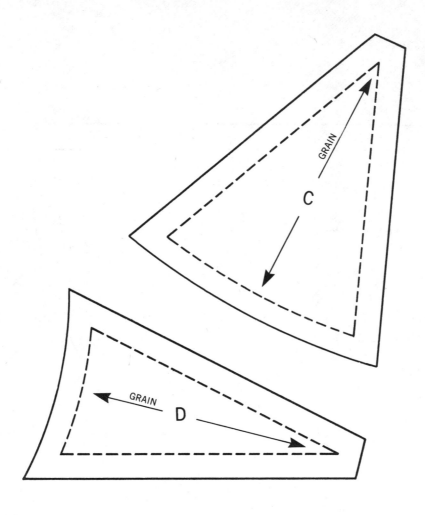

GRAIN

C

GRAIN

D

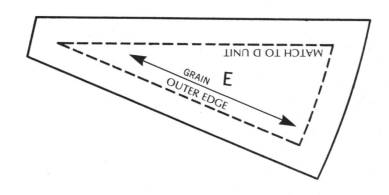

MATCH TO D UNIT

GRAIN

OUTER EDGE

E

Patchwork Flower

With a bright yellow print for sashing and backing, these flowers would gladden any room. Make the centers yellow and the leaves and stems green, and use a different print for the petals of each flower. To make the quilt really come alive, have half the flowers face one way and half the other. Alternate rows.

Blocks: 11 by 13 inches

Quilt top: 70 by 95½ inches with 2½-inch sashing and border
30 blocks

Material you will need
Yellow for center A units: ⅛ yard
Prints for petal B units: 6- by 10-inch piece for each block or 1⅜ yards for all 30 blocks (⅛ yard will be enough for 3 blocks)
Green for leaves and stem: 1 yard
Tan for background squares: 3¾ yards
Print for sashing: 2¾ yards, plus 5⅜ yards for matching back if desired
Black embroidery floss

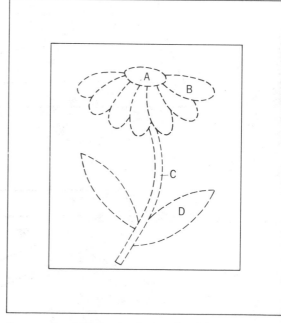

Each block requires
Yellow: 1 unit A
Print: 7 unit B
Green: 1 unit C
         2 unit D
Tan: 1 piece 11½ by 13½ inches

Finished quilt requires
Yellow: 30 unit A
Prints: 30 sets unit B (210 unit B)

See pages 9 and 10 for color photographs of this quilt.

Green: 30 unit C
60 unit D
Tan: 30 pieces 11½ by 13½
inches
Sashing and border: 24 pieces
3 by 13½ inches
5 pieces 3 by 65½ inches
2 pieces 3 by 70½ inches+
2 pieces 3 by 96 inches +

Special cutting notes
Cut sashing fabric, 2¾ yards, in
twelve 3-inch-wide strips the full
length of the fabric. Cut the nine
long strips required for your
quilt from nine of the extra long
strips. From the remaining
strips, cut the twenty-four 13½-
inch-long strips.
Make certain you include a
seam allowance when you cut
the unit C pieces.

To make one block
Place stem on background square,
about ½ inch from the bottom
edge, and position the two D
units (the leaves) on either side,
with the ends tucked under the
stem. Place the B units above the
stem, with each petal overlapping the one before it, pointing
in the direction away from the
bottom of the stem. Then place
the A unit on top of the B units.
Baste in place and then sew.
Outline all pieces with a running
stitch using 4 strands of black
embroidery thread to emphasize
the pattern. Press when completed.

To assemble the quilt top
Join the flower blocks in rows of
five blocks each alternating with
four pieces of sashing, width of
quilt. Make six of these. Now
join these six rows to each other
alternating with the five pieces
of sashing 3 by 65½ inches. Now
join the border strips and miter
the corners.

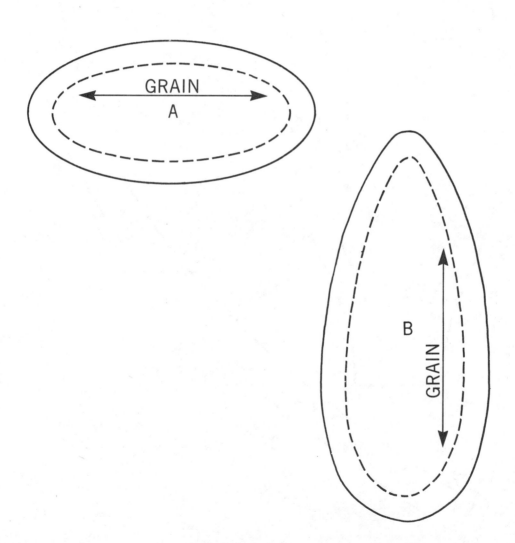

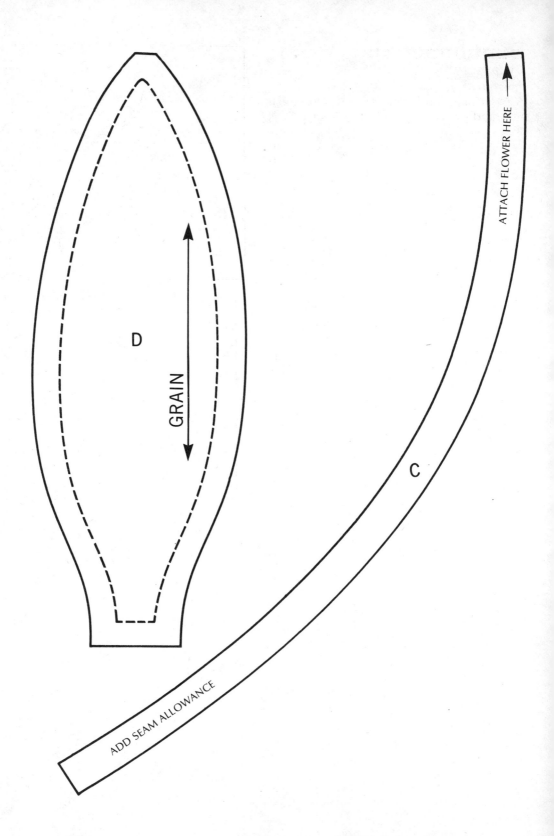

D

GRAIN

C

ATTACH FLOWER HERE

ADD SEAM ALLOWANCE

Sunbonnet Sue

A most delightful design, especially for a little girl's room. One interesting feature that makes this pattern even more lovely is that the colors for the dress units can be varied, giving you a change of materials to work on.

Blocks: 17½ inches square

Quilt top: 70 by 87½ inches
20 blocks

Material you will need
Blue for A (pocket), C, G, H and I (bonnet ribbons) and F units (shoes): ½ yard
White for B unit (arm): piece 9 by 11 inches
Solid color for D unit (bonnet): piece 5 by 5½ inches for each block; ½ yard for entire quilt
Print for E unit (dress): piece 7 inches square for each block; ½ yard for entire quilt
Green for J (stems) and K units (leaves): ¼ yard
Blue print for L (flowers) and M units (centers): ⅛ yard
Red print for L and M units: ⅛ yard
White or other light color for background squares: 5 yards
Embroidery floss

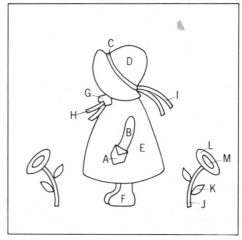

Each block requires
Blue:	1 unit A
	1 unit C
	2 unit F
	2 unit G
	2 unit H
	2 unit I
White:	1 unit B
Solid:	1 unit D
Print:	1 unit E
Green:	2 unit J
	4 unit K
Blue print:	1 unit L
	1 unit M
Red print:	1 unit L
	1 unit M
White:	1 18-inch square

Finished quilt top requires
Blue:	20 unit A
	20 unit C
	40 unit F
	20 unit G
	40 unit H
	40 unit I
White:	20 unit B
Solid:	20 unit D
Print:	20 unit E
Green:	40 unit J
	80 unit K
Blue print:	20 unit L
	20 unit M
Red print:	20 unit L
	20 unit M
White:	20 18-inch squares

Special cutting note
Use the half E unit pattern to make
a full size pattern before cutting
the fabric rather than cut fabric
on the fold.

To make one block

Appliqué an arm and pocket unit to dress; press. Appliqué the flower centers to the flower u-nits, alternating the colors, and press again. Now apply the bonnet band to the bonnet and one shoe on top of the other, ¼ inch lower and ¼ inch to the right; press these sections.

Crease the block once down the middle. Use this center crease as a guideline to put "Sue" in the middle of the block.

Place the shoe units at the center base of the background, 2¼ inches from the bottom edge. The dress unit is placed just above the shoes and the bonnet unit at the top of the dress, with the bow and front tie units (G and H units) at the front where the bonnet and dress meet and the back streamers (I units) at the back end of the bonnet band. The stem units are placed to the left and right of the figure, 4¼ inches from the bottom edge. The flower units are then placed at the top of the stem units and the leaves at the left and right of the stems.

Now baste all units into place and hemstitch into position. The touches of embroidery or other trim on the pocket and other places can be added as you wish. Use 4 strands of embroidery floss. Press the block when completed.

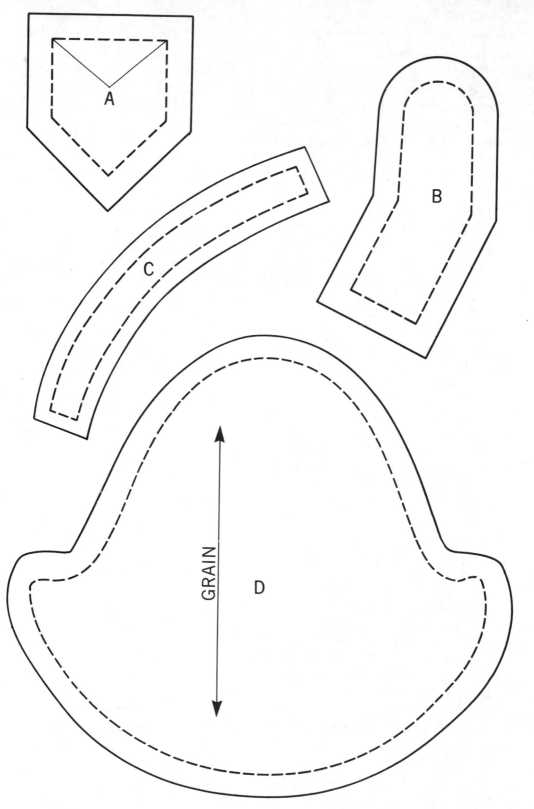

A

B

C

GRAIN

D

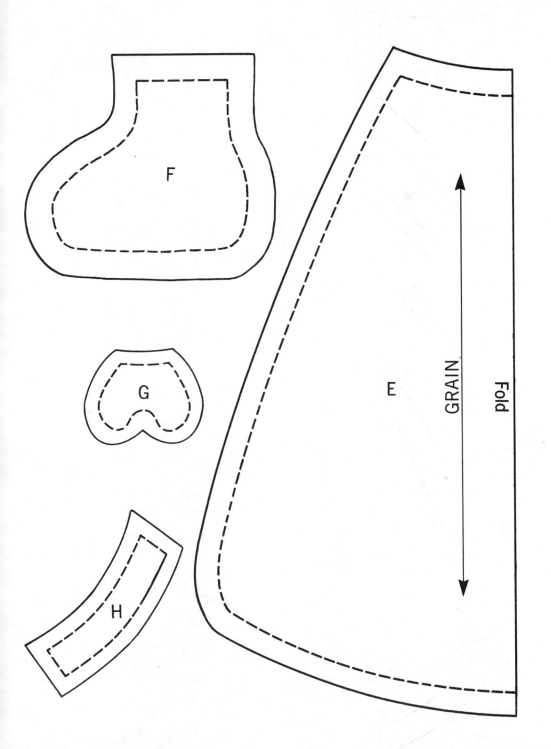

F

G

H

E

GRAIN

Fold

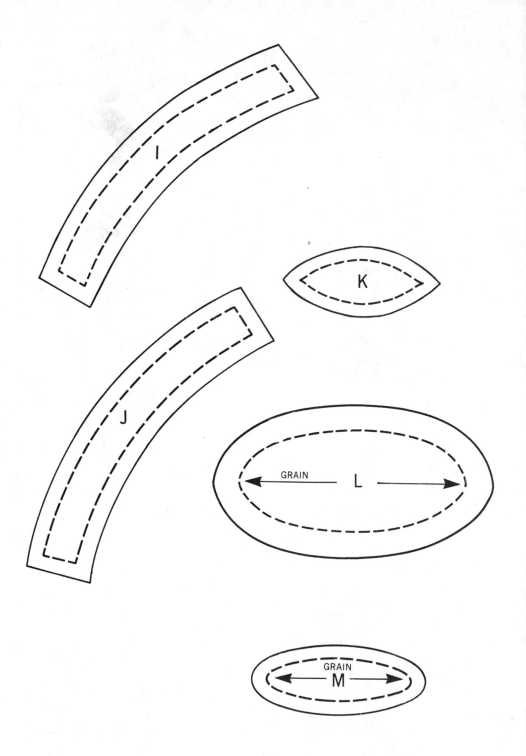

Wild Rose

The rose has always been a popular flower to use as a quilt pattern. Its red, pink and green colors are as refreshing and charming as the rose itself. No one will ever regret the time involved in making this pattern into a beautiful coverlet. It will be a source of comfort and delight for years to come.

Blocks: 17½ inches square

Quilt top: 70 by 87½ inches
20 blocks

Material you will need
Red for A units: 1 yard
Green for B, C, E and F units: 3¼
  yards
Pink for D units: ½ yard
White for background squares: 5
  yards

Each block requires
Red: 4 unit A
Green: 20 unit B
          8 unit C
          8 unit E
          4 unit F
Pink: 8 unit D
White: 1 18-inch square

Finished quilt requires
Red: 80 unit A
Green: 400 unit B
         160 unit C
         160 unit E
          80 unit F
Pink: 160 unit D
White: 20 18-inch squares

To make one block

Crease the background block twice dividing it into quarters, top to bottom and side to side. Use these creases to guide in the placement of pieces, especially the F units. Place the A units in a circle at the center of the background square, with an F unit stem at the top, left, right and bottom of the circle. Five leaves (B units) are placed on each stem, two near the center circle and three at the end. Two E unit stems are then placed on each F unit stem, with a C and then a D unit at the end of each. Baste all units into position and then hemstitch to background; press when completed.

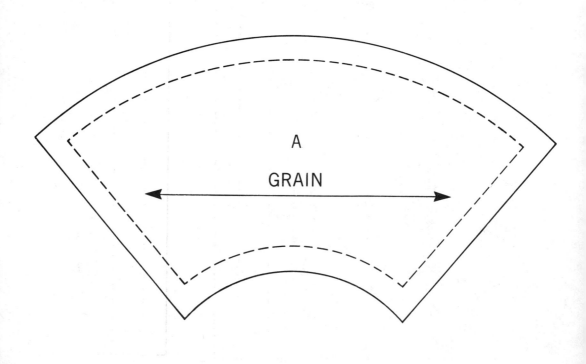

A

GRAIN

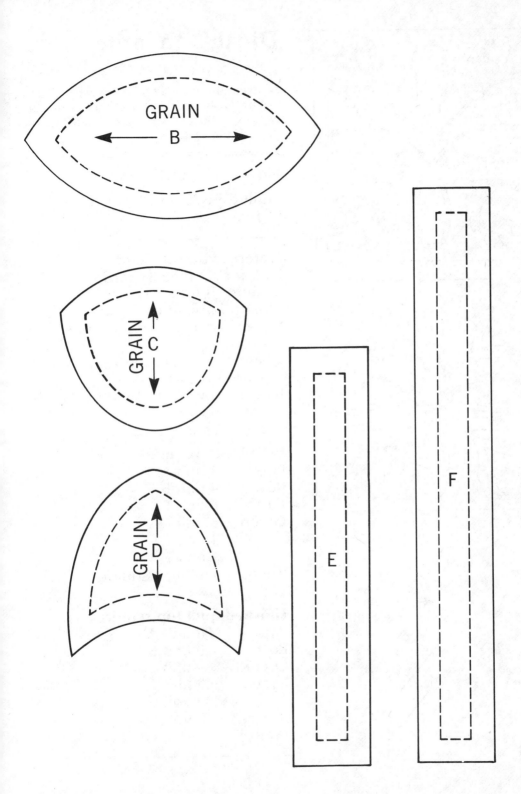

GRAIN B

GRAIN C

GRAIN D

E

F

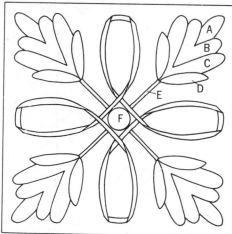

Dinah's Favorite

To make this quilt a real prize winner, use bright, vivid colors. This attractive design will give you enjoyment and satisfaction in both the making and the using.

Blocks: 17½ inches square

Quilt top: 70 by 87½ inches
20 blocks

Material you will need
Pink for A units: ½ yard
Rose for B units: 1¼ yards
Orchid for C units: 3 yards
Green for D, E and F units: 1¼ yards
White for background squares: 5 yards
Blue narrow seam binding or ribbon: 50 yards

Each block requires
Pink: 4 unit A
Rose: 4 unit B
Orchid: 4 unit C
Green: 8 unit D
          4 unit E
          1 unit F
White: 1 18-inch square

Finished quilt top requires
Pink: 80 unit A
Rose: 80 unit B
Orchid: 80 unit C
Green: 160 unit D
          80 unit E
          20 unit F
White: 20 18-inch squares

To make one block

Crease the background block top to bottom, side to side, and diagonally corner to corner twice to guide the placement of pieces and ribbon as shown in the illustrations.

Apply a B unit to an A unit; press each piece as it is joined. Then add on a C unit, then a D unit on the left and right of the C unit. Press. Make four of these sections and place them in the corners of the background square. The F unit is placed in the center and the four E units connecting the center and corner units. Cut 7½ feet of seam binding and loop it around between the corner sections as in the diagram. Baste all units into place and appliqué to background with a hemming stitch. Press when completed.

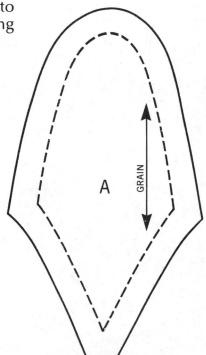

A

GRAIN

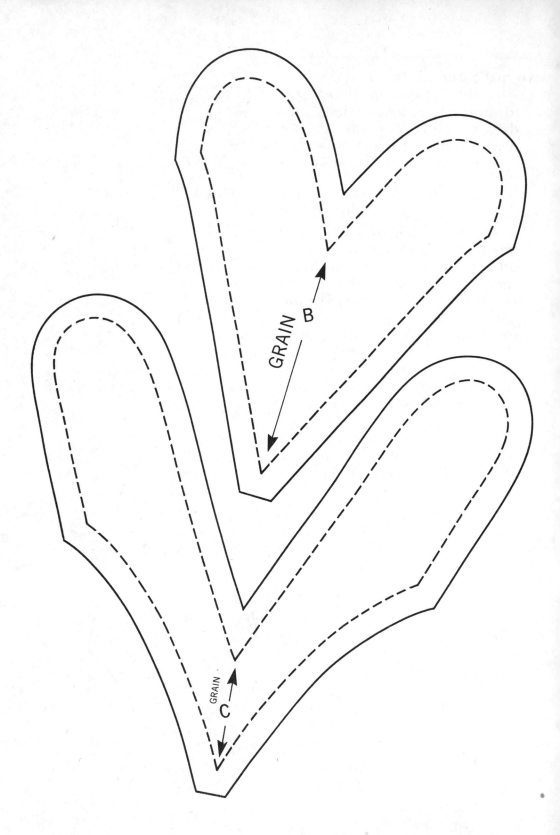

GRAIN B

GRAIN C

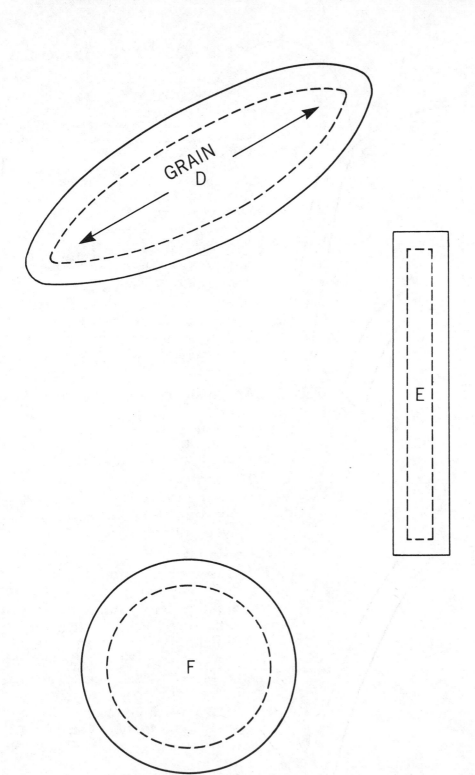

GRAIN
D

E

F

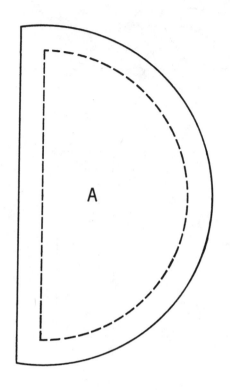

A

Pennies From Heaven

This design has ever so many good points. All odd scrap pieces, large or small, can be used — one of a kind or as many of the same color as you like. There are no guides to follow. The design is a brand-new one to the quilt world, and the very first appearance of a finished "Pennies from Heaven" quilt brought its owner a blue ribbon.

Different from most quilts, this one is made all in one piece. For a 71-by-90-inch quilt top, it will require five yards of material for the background, cut in half crosswise and then sewn together with a center seam.

Approximate number of pieces required
 90 unit A
275 unit B
175 unit C
275 unit D
These figures will vary depending on your choice of distance between pennies.

To assemble the quilt top
Before beginning to appliqué the pennies onto your quilt top, it will help to place basting stitches or light pencil lines on the top to serve as a guide for each of the areas. Area A should measure 2 inches wide from the cut edges. Area B is 14 inches wide, and area C is 9 inches wide. Area D will measure about 22 by 40 inches.

Begin by appliquéing the A units around the edges to form a border. Place 20 A units across the top and bottom and 25 A units down each side. They should be of many different colors and designs. Inside the border, apply four rows of B units, placing them in a hit-and-miss fashion. Follow this with three rows of C units and then fill the center space with the small D units.

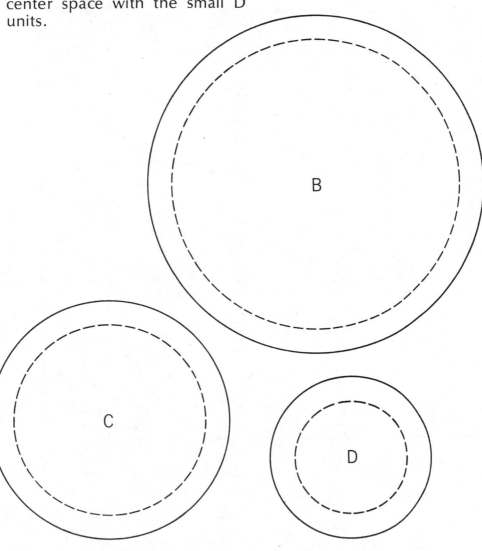

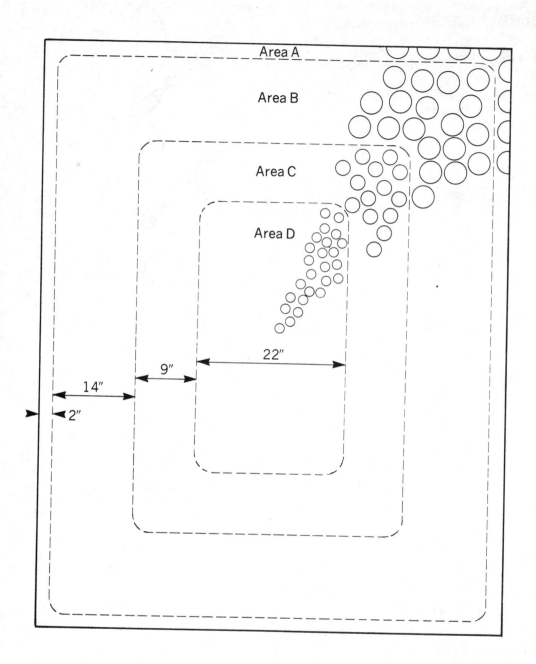

Job's Tears

Another odd-scrap design that adds new interest plus beauty to quiltmaking. One of the easiest patterns imaginable, it can be made either in blocks or as an overall design, though it is easier to handle in blocks. The array of colors makes it delightful to work on. Use a dark print or solid for the centers, a light color background and assorted gay prints for the petals. A border is not required, but if one is desired it can be made of plain material 3 inches wide. For a more decorative border you can cut half petal units and appliqué them to a 3-inch-wide strip of the background material.

Blocks: 11½ inches square

Quilt top: 69 by 92 inches
48 blocks

Material you will need
Dark print for centers: ½ yard
Assorted prints for petals: for each,
   a piece 5 by 2 inches
Total yardage for B units: 3¼ yards
Light color for background: 5⅓
   yards

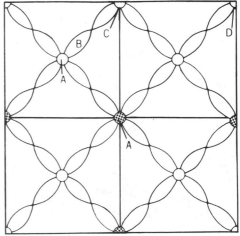

See page 8 for color photograph of this quilt.

Each block requires
Dark print: 1 unit A
                    4 unit C
Assorted prints: 8 unit B
Background: 1 12-inch square

Finished quilt requires
Dark print: 83 unit A
                   28 unit C
Assorted prints: 384 unit B
Background: 48 12-inch squares

To make one block

Crease the block twice diagonally corner to corner. Use these creases to correctly place the B units.

Place the eight B units diagonally across the background square and position the A unit in the center, overlapping the B units. Baste and hemstitch in place. Press when completed and join blocks to complete the quilt top.

When the quilt top is completed, position and stitch A units at each place where the blocks meet. Also position and stitch a C unit at each corner, trimming off the excess.

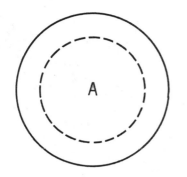

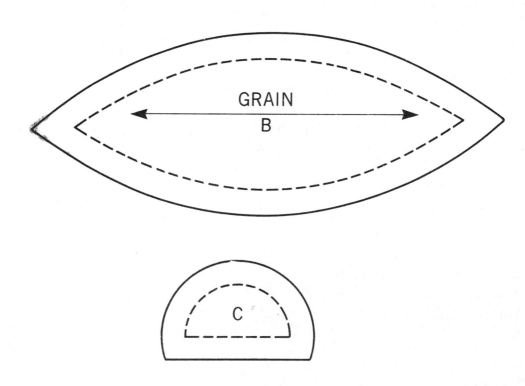

Seashore Quilt

Just the pattern for that fisherman — he can have his own quilt, just to his liking. Shades of lavender may be all wrong for leaves and seaweed, but nevertheless that is what the designer ordered.

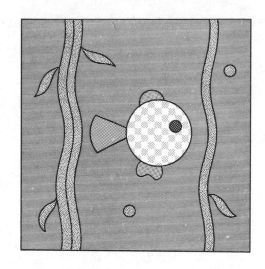

Blocks: 14 inches square

Quilt top: 70 by 98 inches
35 blocks

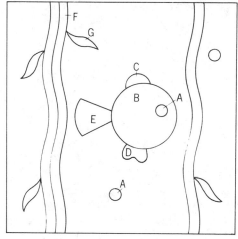

Material you will need

Red for A units: piece 7 inches square

Lavender for A, F and G units: 2 yards

Yellow and white checked for B units: ¾ yard

Orange for C, D and E units: ½ yard

Green for background squares: 7¼ yards

Each block requires

Red:	1	unit A
Lavender:	2	unit A
	3	unit F
	4	unit G
Checked:	1	unit B
Orange:	1	unit C
	1	unit D
	1	unit E
Green:	1	14½-inch square

Finished quilt top requires

Red:	35	unit A
Lavender:	70	unit A
	105	unit F
	140	unit G

Checked:	35 unit B
Orange:	35 unit C
	35 unit D
	35 unit E
Green:	35 unit 14½-inch squares

Special cutting notes

Use the half F unit pattern to make a full size pattern before cutting the fabric rather than cut the fabric on the fold.

If you should decide to make the left two F units just one double wide unit, make a pattern accordingly.

To make one block

Appliqué the red A unit to the B unit and press. Place this unit in the center right of the background square. The C, D and E units are then placed at the top, bottom and left side of the B unit to make a fish with fins and tail. An F unit is then placed at the nose end of the fish, and then the other two F units next to each other at an equal distance from the left edge. Care should be taken that the F units are placed the same on each block so they will match and form continuous vertical lines when the quilt top is assembled. If you wish you may cut this as a double-wide F unit instead. The G units are placed to the left and right of the F units, and the lavender A units can be placed wherever it suits your fancy;

there is no set rule to follow. After all units are in place, baste and then stitch to background square. Press when completed.

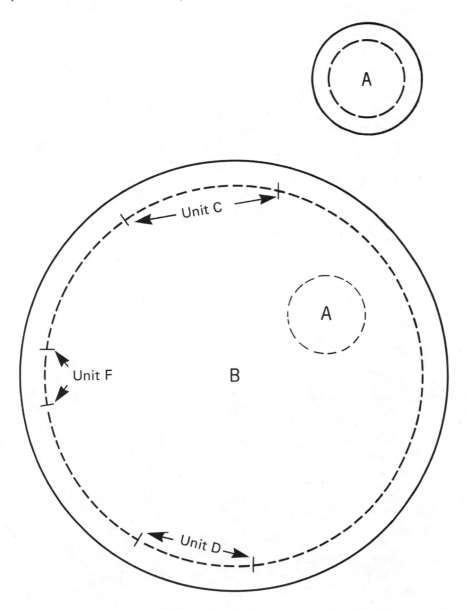

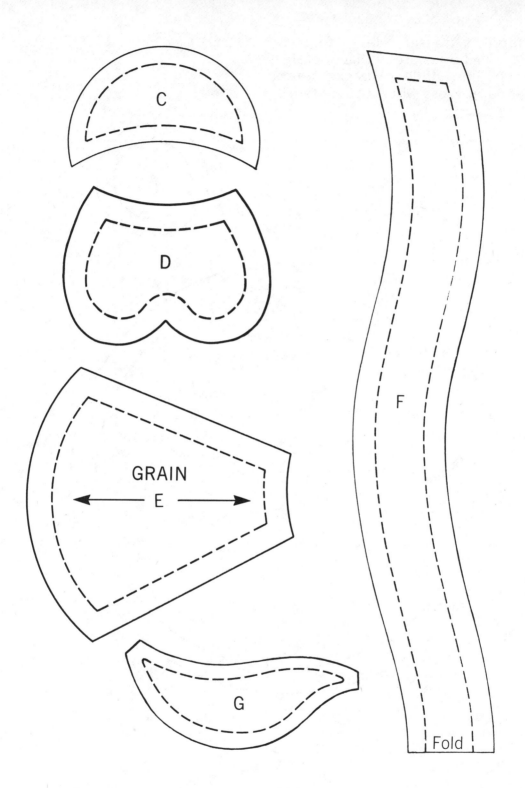

C

D

GRAIN

E

F

G

Fold

Print Dahlia

Only the dahlia can give us this large, bold design that will bring all the glory and grace of the garden into our rooms. A striking design that will demand attention and admiration from all.

Blocks: 17½ inches square

Quilt top: 70 by 87½ inches
20 blocks

Material you will need
Orange for A and D units: ½ yard
Print for B and E units: 2¼ yards
Green for C units: ½ yard
White for background squares: 5 yards
Green ribbon or bias tape: 45 yards

Each block requires
Orange: 1 unit A
           4 unit D
Print: 9 unit B
           12 unit E
Green: 8 unit C
White: 1 18-inch square

Finished quilt top requires
Orange: 20 unit A
           80 unit D
Print: 180 unit B
           240 unit E
Green: 160 unit C
White: 20 18-inch squares

To make one block
Prepare the background block by creasing it top to bottom, side to side, and diagonally corner to

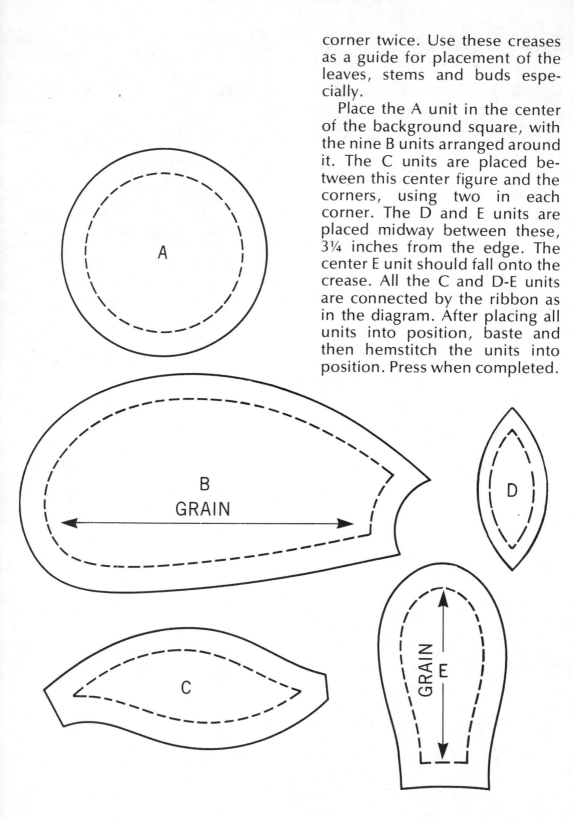

corner twice. Use these creases as a guide for placement of the leaves, stems and buds especially.

Place the A unit in the center of the background square, with the nine B units arranged around it. The C units are placed between this center figure and the corners, using two in each corner. The D and E units are placed midway between these, 3¼ inches from the edge. The center E unit should fall onto the crease. All the C and D-E units are connected by the ribbon as in the diagram. After placing all units into position, baste and then hemstitch the units into position. Press when completed.

A

B
GRAIN

D

C

GRAIN
E

The Dutch Mill

For those who wish to remember their first sight of a Dutch mill, or for those who just like outdoor scenes, no design could be better. Its simple lines make it pleasant to do.

Blocks: 17½ inches

Quilt top: 70 by 87½ inches
20 blocks

Material you will need
Tan print for A units: ¾ yard
Red for B and C units: ¼ yard
Red and white checked for D units: ½ yard
Yellow for E units: ⅝ yard
Blue for background squares: 5 yards
2 skeins black embroidery floss

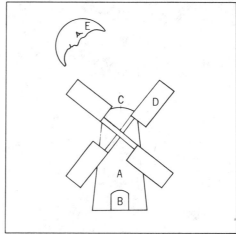

Each block requires
Tan: 1 unit A
Red: 1 unit B
            2 unit C
Checked: 4 unit D
Yellow: 1 unit E
Blue: 1 18-inch square

Finished quilt top requires
Tan: 20 unit A
Red: 20 unit B
            40 unit C
Checked: 80 unit D
Yellow: 20 unit E
Blue: 20 18-inch squares

To make one block

Apply the B unit to the A unit and then place this section in the center of the background square, 1¾ inches from the bottom edge. The C units are then placed in an X position across the A unit, 2 inches down from the top of the unit, and a D unit is placed at each end. The E unit is placed 2 inches from the top edge to the left of center, face downward. Baste all units into place and hemstitch. With the black floss, embroider a face on the moon. Press when completed.

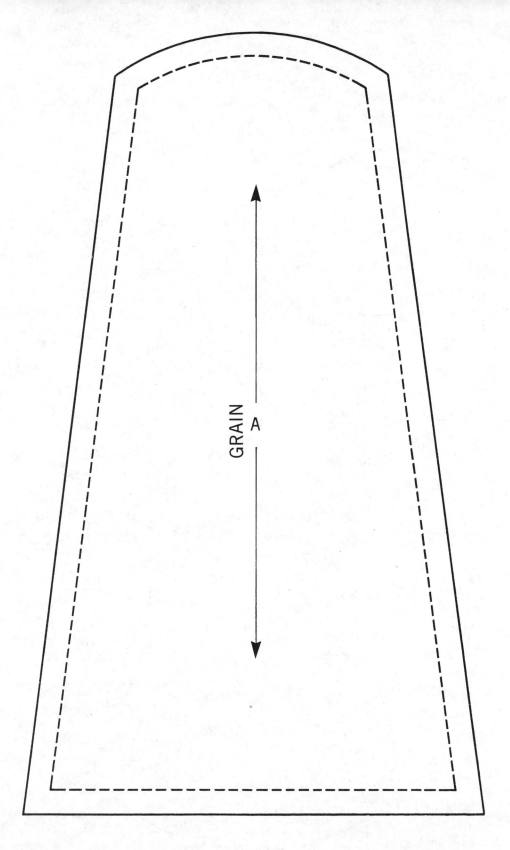

GRAIN

A

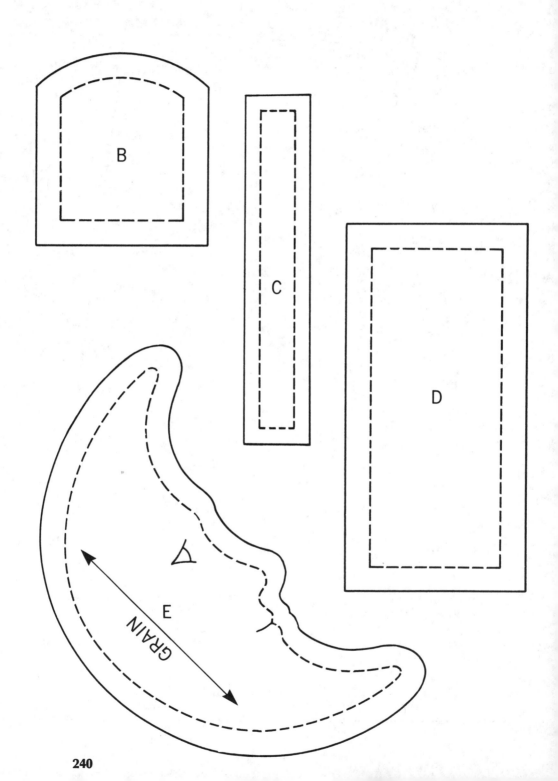

B

C

D

E

GRAIN

Rose of Sharon

One of the loveliest of the older patterns, it is a design that demands time and exactness. It is more intricate than most appliquéd designs but the finished quilt will repay the maker a hundredfold in pleasure and satisfaction.

This is always at its best when made of a light shade of green and a deep red.

Blocks: 17½ inches square

Quilt: 70 by 87½ inches
20 blocks

Material you will need
Red for A, B, G and H units: ¾ yard
Green for C, D, E, F and I units: 3¼ yards
White for background squares: 5 yards

Each block requires
Red: 1 unit A
           1 unit B
           4 unit G
           4 unit H
Green: 4 unit C
           4 unit D
           4 unit E
           4 unit F
        16 unit I
White: 1 18-inch square

Finished quilt requires
Red: 20 unit A
          20 unit B
          80 unit G
          80 unit H
Green: 80 unit C
          80 unit D

80 unit E
80 unit F
320 unit I

White: 20 18-inch squares

To make one block

Prepare the background block by creasing it top to bottom, side to side, and diagonally corner to corner twice. Use these creases as a guide for placement of the A, C and D units especially.

Place the A unit in center of background with the B unit surrounding it. Now place C units at the edge of the B unit, with points facing toward the corners of the background square. Line them up with the diagonal creases. The D units are placed between the C units, at the other four creases, with one F unit and one G unit at the ends. Make certain you put the correct end of the D unit to the B unit. The E units are positioned branching off the D units, with the H units at the ends. The I units are placed to the left and right of the D and E units. Baste all units into position and hemstitch into place. Press when completed.

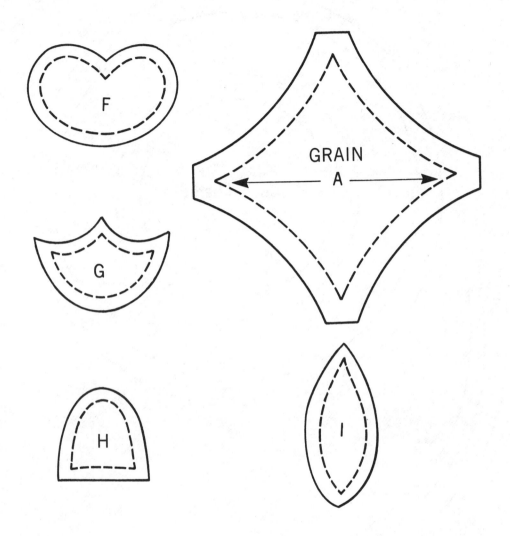

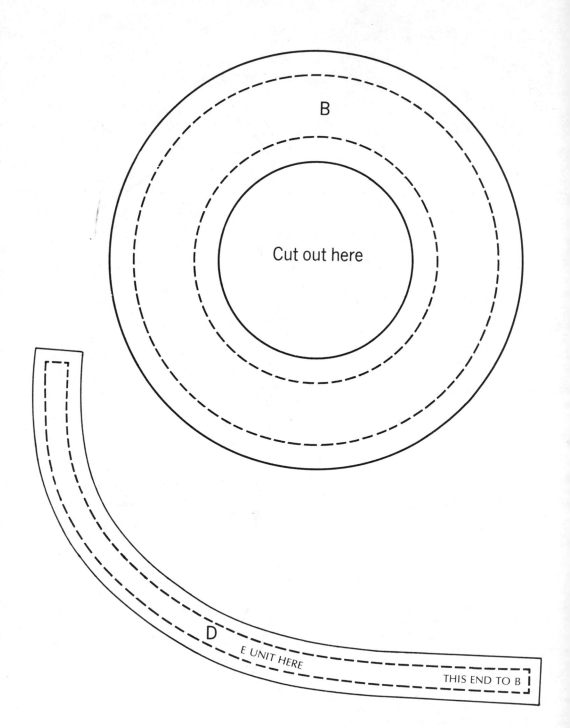

B

Cut out here

D

E UNIT HERE

THIS END TO B

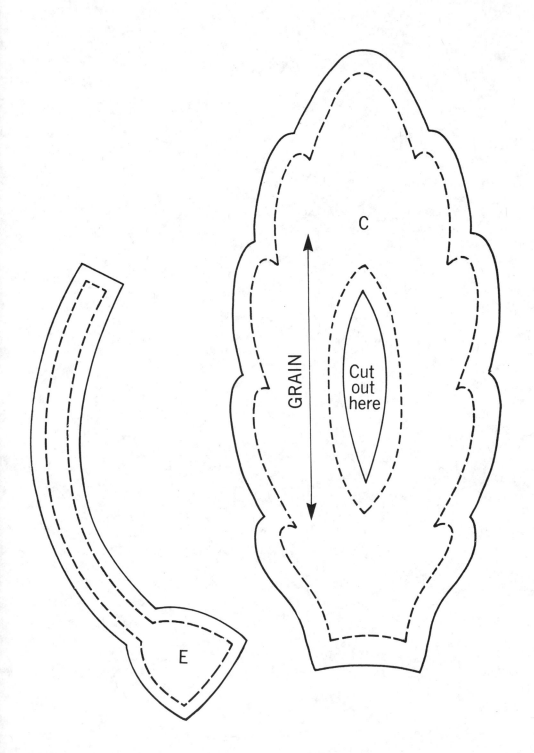

C

GRAIN

Cut
out
here

E

BORDERS

Plain Diamond Border

This is the simplest border one could choose, yet its many color combinations will add prestige and beauty to any coverlet. Use all diffent scraps for the A units if you wish, or you may want them all the same, perhaps of a different print from any used in the general makeup of the quilt. The good point of this design is that the units may repeat or contrast with the colors that you have used in the main quilt.

In any event the color arrangement will require about ¾ yard of material for each color (based on using 2 colors for diamonds and 1 color for triangles) to complete the border for the average-sized coverlet. The finished border measures 2¾ inches wide and repeats every 2 inches.

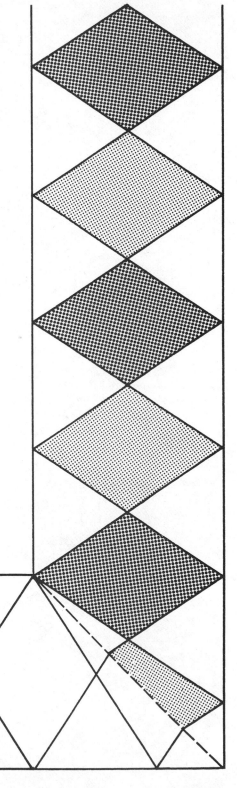

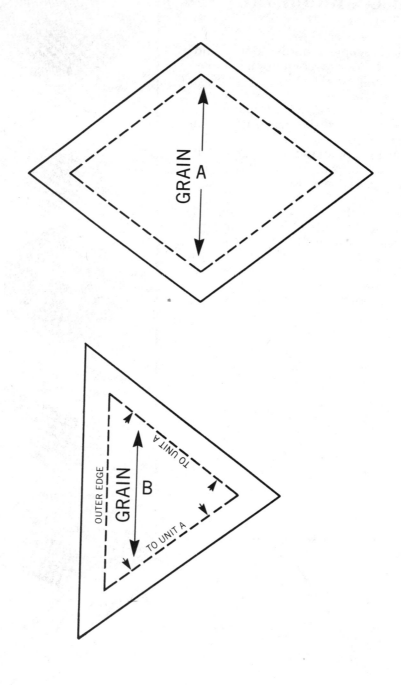

Zig-Zag Border

This border design may be employed in two ways. The B and C units may be joined to form rows the length and width of your coverlet and applied over the outer edge. Or, if another color is desired, the A units are used to join the sections made by combining the B and C units. One-third yard of material of each color will be required for the border for an average-sized quilt. Make rows the length and width of your quilt top plus twice the width of the border. These rows are then joined to the outer edges of the quilt and the corners are mitered.

The finished border measures 5½ inches wide and repeats every 3½ inches.

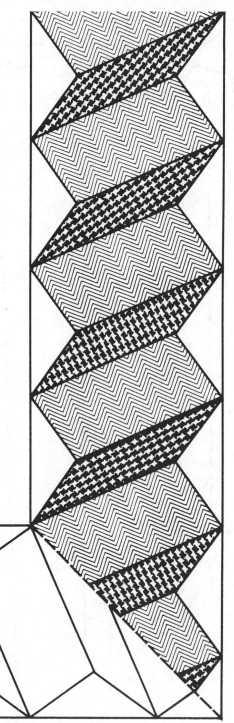

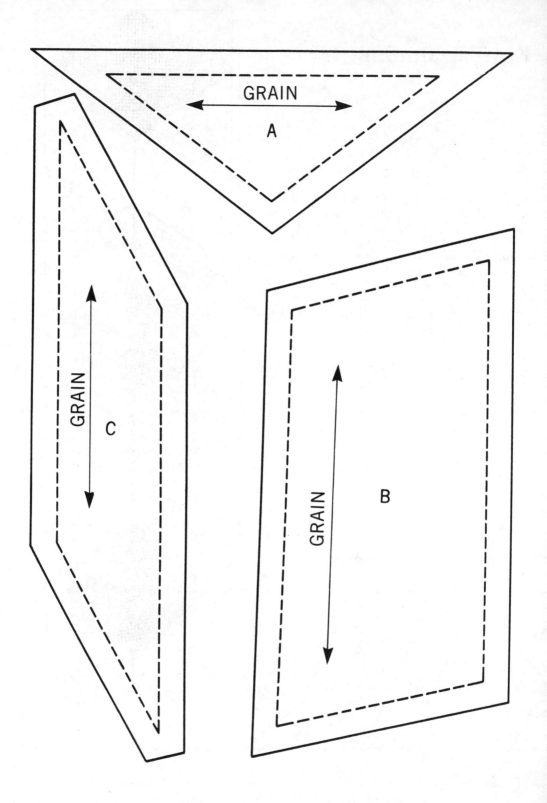

GRAIN

A

GRAIN

C

GRAIN

B

Fancy Diamond Border

This border is at its best when a definite color arrangement is used. The B units are usually of the same color as the main color or background of the quilt. The A units are usually all alike, and the C units are usually of scrap pieces.

For the average 72-by-90-inch quilt, ¾ yard of material will be sufficient for the A units and ⅓ yard for the B units. You will need a piece 3 by 3½ inches to cut two C units, one facing left and one facing right.

To make the border, join two sets of C units to the sides of the A unit and press. Place the B units between each of the sections made. Make rows the length and width of your quilt top plus twice the width of the border. These rows are then joined to the outer edges of the quilt and the corners are mitered. The finished border measures 3 inches wide and repeats every 4 inches.

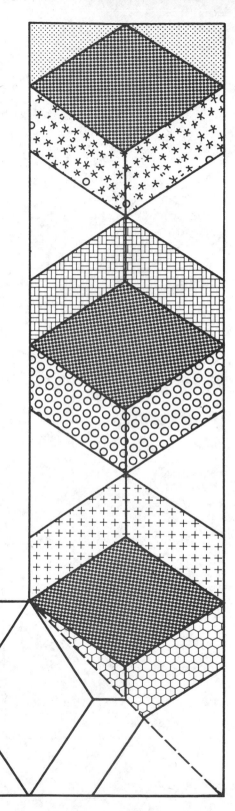

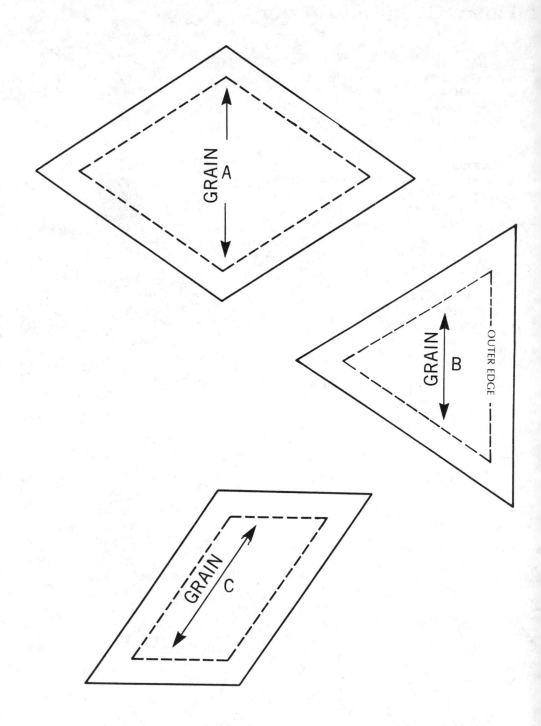

Flowered Border

This appliquéd border should be done in three colors.

For a quilt 72 by 90 inches you require 11 yards of bias binding for the vine, 1 yard of material for the A units, ⅓ yard for the B units and ⅔ yard for the C units.

Place the bias binding on the background, two inches from the quilt edge at the narrowest point and four inches at the widest. Baste. This same procedure may be used when a plain border at least 6 inches wide has been added to the quilt. The B units are appliquéd to the center of all C units and these flowers are then placed at intervals of ten inches along the entire length of the vine. The A units are placed along the vine, with three at the inner and four at the outer edge, in alternating positions.

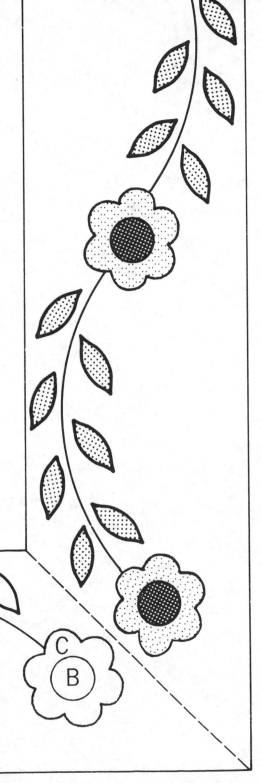

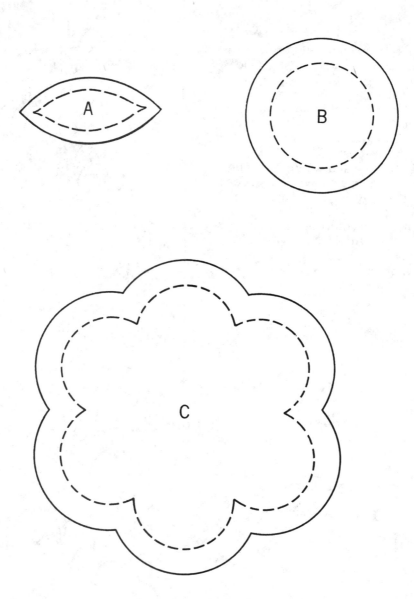

A

B

C

Scalloped Border

This border looks very well if its design is placed some distance from the outer edge of the quilt. The border will be six inches wide, and a space of four inches should be allowed between the scallops and any part of the main section of the quilt.

For a 72-by-90-inch quilt you will need 2½ yards of light-colored background material, 1 yard of a solid color for the A units, 3½-inch-square scraps for the B units, and ⅓ yard of green for the C units. Cut the border strips lengthwise of the fabric; two strips 6½ by 90½ inches and two strips 6½ by 72½ inches. Attach these border strips to the main section of the quilt top (60½ by 78½ inches) and miter the corners.

The A units are now basted into position at the outer edge of the border. The B units are next placed just above and between each A unit and likewise basted into place. These are now backstitched and pressed. The C units are placed at the top of each B unit at a slight angle pointing toward the top of the border. There are many variations as to the placing of the C units. Beside the placement shown here, you could put a cluster of three C units in the valley between the B units or you could eliminate the C units altogether.

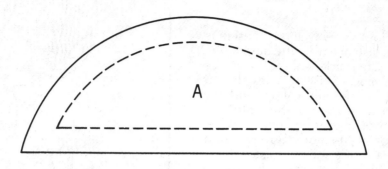

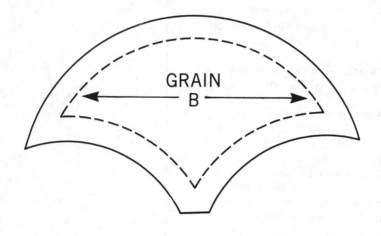

GRAIN
B

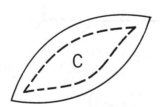

Angle Border

This easily made border can be created from odd scraps of material, or only two colors may be used throughout. Only one cutting unit is needed. It should be cut left and right so the patterns are not reversed when the units are joined.

For a 72-by-90-inch quilt, if just two colors are used you will need 1 yard of each, to cut 108 units of each color. Alternatively, a total of 216 odd-scrap pieces will be needed.

To make the border, first piece the units into rectangles of two units each. Then assemble the rectangles — twenty-four for the top and bottom and thirty for each side — and join together. The finished border measures 4 inches wide and repeats every 3 inches.

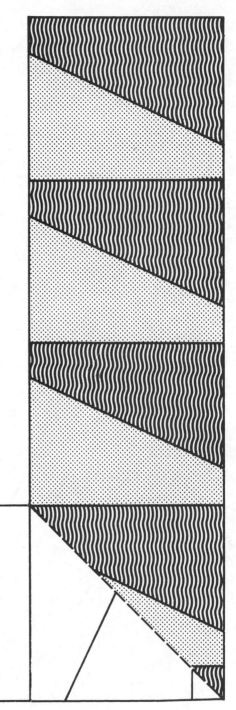

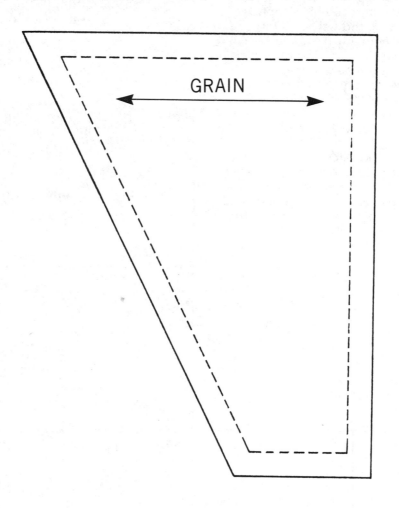

GRAIN